THE WAVES

Demystifying the Human Experience

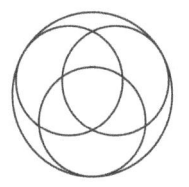

Kaya Usher

The Waves
Copyright © 2023 by Kaya Usher

All rights reserved. No part of this publication may be reproduced, distributed, or transmitted in any form or by any means, including photocopying, recording, or other electronic or mechanical methods, without the prior written permission of the author, except in the case of brief quotations embodied in critical reviews and certain other non-commercial uses permitted by copyright law.

tellwell

Tellwell Talent
www.tellwell.ca

ISBN
978-1-77941-371-0 (Hardcover)
978-1-77941-369-7 (Paperback)
978-1-77941-370-3 (eBook)

ACKNOWLEDGEMENTS

"I would like to thank God, our Creator of all there is for showing me the way Home. I would also like to thank my beautiful friend Jacalyn Burke for bringing this book to life. I would like to thank all of you who are here right now and have chosen this path back to your Brilliant Self. In particular, those of our Holy Order.

The Waves augments the 8 Tenets, demystifying our human experience through sanctification. We are blessed."

Kaya Usher

INTRODUCTION

The Waves is a body of knowledge that was revealed to Kaya Usher in 2022. It is designed to demystify the human experience, teaching us how our human body is divinely structured and why it was created in the first place.

This book uses the third person narrative throughout, i.e. using "we" instead of "I" and referring to Kaya Usher in the third person as the Teacher. Primarily, this is done because this is how the information was received. We also wanted to offer a sense of distance and objectivity to the information, which we believe bolsters collectivity and inclusion. Ours is not a hierarchical structure as Tenet 5 attests.

> Live Free To Be
> "We do not operate from old paradigms. We are free of rituals, rites, orders and rank. We commune in equality. There is no hierarchy."

Moreover, our intention is to enable the student's exploration using multiple perspectives and angles, adding depth to their experience.

Throughout this book you will learn why you are here in human form and how that relates to everything else. As you uncover your truth you will naturally return to a state of reverence and awe for the Intelligence behind YOU. This is an act of sanctification.

We recommend that students also experience The Waves as a pre-recorded video course taught by Kaya Usher. It is available for purchase here: thesimplicityplatform.com/store.

In the video course you will experience Kaya's unique teaching style which utilizes activating Frequencies through the spoken word. This book has also been especially encoded with Frequency-activating words. It's the Frequencies that do the work.

The information delivered in this book is holographic by format. This means that each Section, each chapter is an echo of another. At times, this may be experienced as repetitive from our linear, third-dimensional perspective.

There are two reasons for this: the most important aspects of this book are repeated in a cyclical manner to generate a resonance that informs us on these levels: mental, emotional, physical, energetic and spiritual; and because this is how the body of knowledge was received.

This material may even feel back to front at times. This is intentional because these teachings resemble a spiral. One that slowly unfolds, like a divine orbit.

We invite you to experience the information offered here in waves, as a spiral unfoldment and as a series of interlocking cycles. There are places within this book that invite us to pause, to ponder, to make notes and to generate our own thoughts (waves) so that an inner dialogue can naturally and spontaneously arise. This is your path - always.

Aids to Comprehension

To get an optimum experience from this book please turn to the back, and read through our guide. We also provide a Glossary of Terms for people new to Kaya Usher's teachings.

If you feel drawn to diving straight in, read on.

TABLE OF CONTENTS

Acknowledgements iii
Introduction v

Section 1
Emergence 1

An Introduction to The Waves 3
Activation: Harmonic Resonance...................................6
The Waves Emerge 12
The Waves and Your Body 15
The Waves and the Cosmos... 28
Activation: Grounding Golden Sovereign Technique..... 42

Section 2
Osmosis 51

Activation: Harmonic Resonance.................................. 53
Blueprint vs Imprint... 56
Free Fall 64
Imprints and Family 74
Fractal, Soul and Avatar 85
The Three Spheres 102

The Principles: Avatar Mechanics 113
Activation: Grounding Golden Sovereign Technique... 124

Section 3
Transfiguration 131

Activation: Harmonic Resonance................................ 133
The Golden Filaments 136
The Waves, You and Everything Else 149
You and God 162
Activation: Grounding Golden Sovereign Technique....172

Book Assets
Closing Thoughts 181
What Others Are Experiencing 189
About Kaya Usher 191
A Guide to Using This Book 193
Glossary of Terms... 201
Diagram List 209
Useful Links 211

Section 1

Emergence

"This is a state of profound self-awareness and observation of previously obscured or hidden elements that require release or integration. These elements arise from our unconscious where humans normally have limited access." Kaya Usher The Waves course

Section 1: Emergence

Contents:

- Harmonic Resonance (opening activation).
- The Waves Emerge.
- The Waves and Your Body.
- The Waves and the Cosmos.
- Grounding Golden Sovereign Technique (closing activation).

An Introduction to The Waves

This book rolls out in three Sections as three Waves:

1. Emergence
2. Osmosis
3. Transfiguration

Through each Section you will learn about your electromagnetic field and how interferences, imprints, and lineages impact it. Understanding how your waves create your reality down to the last detail empowers you. Knowing the difference between a coherent and an incoherent wave will make a profound difference to your life experience.

Coherence is important because it activates our electromagnetic field to resonate in a neutral state. This is the state where the manifestation of all things is possible - instantaneously. It is a space free of attachments and interferences. The infinite, the unimaginable, all spontaneously spring from here and we call such things miracles. As you read further you will come to know why.

Coherence is a fertile bed for manifestation. Kaya Usher calls this Harmonic Resonance.

There is much written about manifestation especially in the realms of healing and material wealth. There are many claims, ideas and personalities that offer the average person access, at a price. The Truth is, if there is a big Secret, you are it; if there's a magic formula, you are it and if there's a hidden society to join, you're already a member.

But don't let that thought solidify. Let it run between your fingers like sand. In fact, you will learn not to attach yourself to anything. We call this Free Fall. Throughout this book you will hear this term often repeated.

Free Fall means to surrender and let go completely. It takes patience, time and commitment because it's a master key.

The ability to Free Fall - at least in the beginning - will come in fits and starts. You may find yourself struggling with letting things go. For example, it may be hard to give up a grudge, especially if the person in question is not sorry for what they've done to us.

Holding onto things is a weight. Whether it be a grudge, a habit, an idea, an addiction, a resentment, an old wound, or an attachment to someone or something. It's normal not to want to let go of what feels familiar or righteously ours. You will in time, come to feel the burden of holding onto such attachments.

They will get heavier the more conscious awareness you bring to their presence. So, as you read on, allow The Waves to run through you, over and over and over again. Offer no resistance. Don't beat yourself up. Keep going.

Everything between these pages begins and ends with You.

The Waves Emerge

"Frequencies vibrate in waves.
We come to resonate this path in Waves."
Kaya Usher Free To Be 365

Activation: Harmonic Resonance

An Opening Activation

We open each of the three Sections of The Waves with a technique that connects you to you, and to others who are engaged in this Frequency Technology practice. We call this activation Harmonic Resonance.

An activation is more than a guided meditation or a mantra. Activations are Frequency coded and they affect our electromagnetic field both consciously and subconsciously.

You can think of the Harmonic Resonance activation as a wave that begins in the heart of the ocean and makes its way to the shore. In between being set in motion it simply rolls, moving everything in its path. When it reaches the coastline it sweeps in, and then according to the tide, it is pulled back out to sea again.

The wave is in constant motion. It is dynamic. It shifts in size and impact, passing through calm waters, through twisting currents and through terrible storms. Yet in the deepest ocean, at its heart and origin point, there is a stillness and calm. The wave carries this stillness and calm with it, throughout its journey.

Likewise, if you do the Harmonic Resonance activation regularly you will create a Frequency pattern (the wave) that produces a continuous coherence. That coherence is internal like the stillness at the ocean's heart.

As of this writing, Harmonic Resonance is the Frequency equivalent of emotional self-regulation. If you prefer not to do it alone, Kaya Usher conducts Harmonic Resonance live every weekday through her community space here: thesimplicityplatform.com/the-simplicity-platform-community.

Harmonic Resonance hones your ability to evoke and sustain a state of deep coherence and peace. Over time you can practice Harmonic Resonance to the point where an Unimaginable Peace becomes your natural state of being. For now, the words used in this book will tune you in.

You may find it useful to record yourself saying the words used in Harmonic Resonance and to play the recording back as many times as you want.

The use of your own voice helps to entrain the conscious part of your mind, which is a gatekeeper of the unconscious. This is important to know because every single distorted program that exists, comes from your unconscious mind.

In summary, we begin each Section of this book with Harmonic Resonance to get you into a state of coherence. It is in this state that you will receive the information more powerfully.

Activation:
Harmonic Resonance

Get comfortable.
Take a few deep breaths in.
You are going to use your breath to take you more deeply into your body.

As you breathe.
Take a few moments to bring your awareness to the surface of your body.
Follow where your awareness goes.
Be guided by your breath.
Be guided by your attention.
(Take a few seconds to settle in)

Now, bring your awareness back to your breath.
Feel your Life Force.
Feel it as it swirls around your body.
Feel your electromagnetic field.
As it resonates around your entire body.
Feel your Frequencies.
As they whirl inside of your body.
(Pause - experience your body)

Now, let's go deeper.
Feel your Frequency system.
It runs all over your body.
It is a luminous network.
It glows.
(Pause - experience your own Frequencies)

Feel your Golden Filaments.

Feel your resonance,
Your heart space,
Spinning brilliantly.
It looks like a golden Sphere.
(Pause - experience your Sphere)

You are not alone.
Others spin.
Your loved ones.
Friends, acquaintances, co-workers, strangers.
Feel how they spin.
Feel the difference between them and you.
Feel that.
Feel your resonance.
Feel theirs.
(Pause - experience their spin)

All the while aware of your spin.
Everyone spins.
It's like a series of golden Spheres.
All spinning at different speeds.
All spinning without order.
They're quite different.
All unique.
Some wobble.
Some spin so fast they move around.
Everyone spins.
Feel that.
(Pause)

Experience the spin, experience the spinning, experience an entire planet filled with humans with spins - all different.
Feel that.

Home.
Back to where you are.
Home.
Back in to the Sphere that is you.
Feel the spin that is you.
(Pause)
Feeling it.

Know - which Spheres are them.
Feel which spins are theirs.
Feel it.

Now feel a magnetism building in your Sphere.
Feel the velocity of your Sphere.
(Pause - experience your own magnetism)

As you bring your awareness into your own spinning Sphere.
You hear a humming like the wings of a hummingbird.
It's faint but it gets stronger and stronger and stronger.
You spin faster and faster and faster.
Faster and stronger and faster and stronger you spin.
Feel a deep vibration building.

There's a flash of light.
Feel that.
Luminous, bright, aglow.
(Pause - feel that light)

You are your own sun.
You resonate so brilliantly.
You are One with the golden spinning Sphere.
Feel yourself Free Fall.
Feel yourself Free Fall into coherence.
(Pause - feel the calm - feel it)

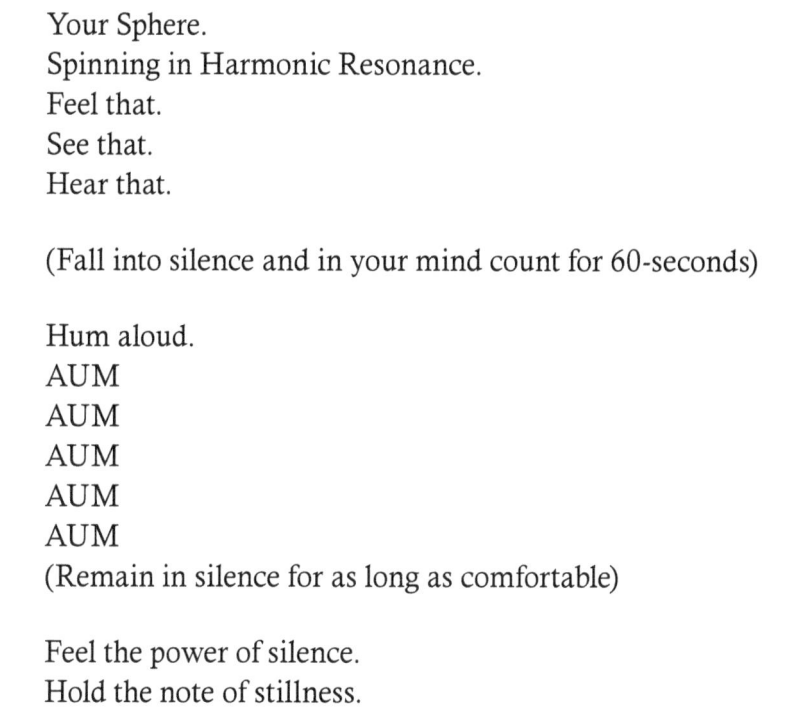

Your Sphere.
Spinning in Harmonic Resonance.
Feel that.
See that.
Hear that.

(Fall into silence and in your mind count for 60-seconds)

Hum aloud.
AUM
AUM
AUM
AUM
AUM
(Remain in silence for as long as comfortable)

Feel the power of silence.
Hold the note of stillness.

This is Harmonic Resonance.
(Repeat as often as required)

The Waves Emerge

This is Truth.
Hear it.

You are made of Frequencies.
Frequencies vibrate in waves.
Waves manifest your realities.
You came to resonate this path in waves.

The Waves is a technology that has always existed but that has remained dormant waiting for activation. Activation is not something someone else can do for you. It is something only you can do. The fact that you are reading this book indicates that activation is now available.

Whether an activation of this technology occurs during the course of you reading this book or at a later date does not matter. Once an awareness of The Waves is set in motion, it will bring your focus to every conscious and unconscious area of your life. This will instigate shifts. If you are not ready to make significant changes, it might be better to put this book down until you are.

What is The Waves?

In layman's terms, The Waves is the ability to bring in and hold more consciousness, especially to the unconscious areas of your existence. Your unconscious nature is the source of your beliefs, habits and desires. It is from this place that your strongest Frequencies emanate. It's the golden goose.

Our thinking (conscious) mind has a lesser effect on our vibrational footprint, the Frequencies we send out through our electromagnetic field. This is because many of our desires, habits and beliefs were formed in early childhood before we had the ability to analyze rationally.

These were imprinted upon us without our consent by well-meaning family members. Some of the imprinting may have been unpleasant and even traumatic. Much of it was unconscious, simply a passed down way of thinking that was acceptable to your family group. This is what drives us 95% of the time. Those drivers become the challenges, the limitations, and the habits that run our lives. In this book we call those things your distortions or programs.

The Waves disrupt all distortions.

How it works

As you read and practice the suggestions in this book, your unconsciousness will be activated. The Waves will call up your distortions, your numerous unconscious aspects, and ask you to look at them. Then you will have a choice to synthesize these formerly lost parts of yourself, and what you cannot synthesize, you can let go of.

We begin with your body.

The Waves and Your Body

This chapter comes in two parts

- Temporal: Your body as a Frequency Technology.
  - Celestial: Your body as Divinely Configured.

The Waves and Your Body

Part 1: Temporal

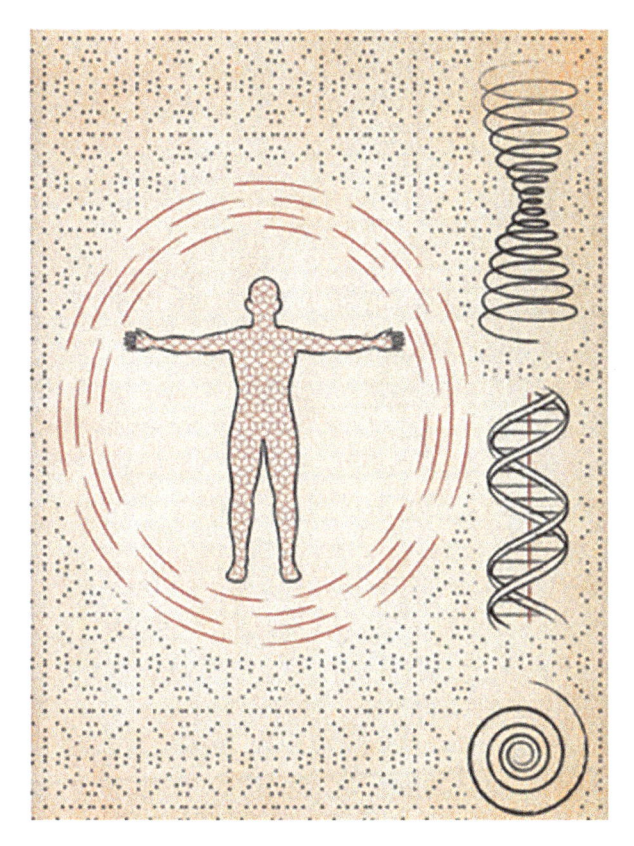

Diagram 1: Frequencies.

Your body doesn't house a Frequency Technology.
Your body is the Frequency Technology.

At arm's length all around you, your body is surrounded by an electromagnetic field. This field contains two primary waves, and they run concurrently.

1. A Push wave (what we signal from us) as thoughts.
2. A Pull wave (what we magnetize to us) as emotions.

These two waves were designed to run simultaneously in Harmonic Resonance.

Push

In its natural pattern our Push wave offers thoughts that ebb and flow as we interact with the world.

However, our culture is obsessed with doers and as children, many of us were taught to always be busy. In fact, we may have been warned against being idle, or of daydreaming too much and were encouraged to be doing something, or to be thinking about something. In time, activities, classes and hobbies created a stream of push, push and push thoughts. That is, anything other than to be still and to go with the flow.

This entrained us to constantly "lean in" on our external world, with an expectation that it satisfies and occupies us. This created an endless stream of thoughts, our own and that of others. This outside-in perspective is unbalanced and it creates interference in our electromagnetic field, and interference leads to incoherence.

Pull

In its natural setting Pull is an attractor of all that is for our highest good.

It's common to think that our conscious mind affects the Law of Attraction, but in fact, it is our unconsciousness that dictates most of what we attract.

The unconscious mind is the source of emotions that can blow in and out like tornadoes. These are the highly emotional and charged impulses of our unconsciousness that erupt like solar flares. They are often primitive, erratic and are behind every impulsive act, misdemeanor or indiscretion.

The unconscious mind is the driver of ego, with its incessant, never satisfied, always seeking more disposition. The unconscious mind fuels our monkey mind. Primal, it is focused on rapidly changing events, jumping from one idea to another but it never settles. It often leaves us scattered and exhausted.

From the chaos of unconsciousness, we layer childhood memories, most of which are formed in the first three years of life. These memories imprint irrational thoughts around every area of a human life. This is the black box, where all of our dreams and nightmares coexist.

Our conscious mind acts as the gatekeeper of our unconsciousness. Preventing us from acting in socially unacceptable, unethical and even illegal ways. But it is not in the driver's seat for the majority of the time. This explains some of the decisions we have impulsively made, and that we came to regret. It explains why we sometimes feel out of control, or feel stuck, or experience (attract) what we don't want more of.

Unconsciousness creates incoherent Push and Pull waves.

On the other hand, if we learn how to stay conscious, which means to remain embodied, in the present-moment, without attachments, and if we live through our heart - *automatically*, there would be a coherence in our electromagnetic field. That is, a natural equilibrium between the Push wave and the Pull wave.

When our Push and Pull waves are in equilibrium, incoherence is replaced by one, interconnected, coherent pulse that signals into the cosmos.

"I AM"
"I AM"
"I AM"

This is Harmonic Resonance and central to it is the human heart.

The heart is more powerful than we can possibly imagine. It is not just an organ and a pump. Your heart holds your Sphere which is your inner sun. Your Sphere contains your Life Force, which is all of the fuel your body will need to keep you alive. It is your connection to Source.

If you could see your Sphere it would resemble a spinning top. This whirling device generates a unique Frequency field that emanates waves. These waves are pulsed from and through your heart. This is how your organ heart receives its charge, which creates a beat. So, the pulse comes first, then the beat, then the flow of blood.

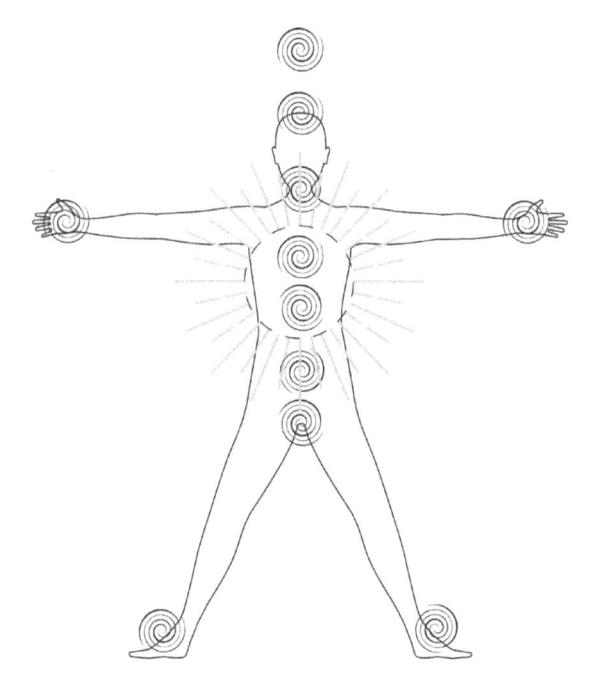

Diagram 2: The body's energy centers.

Within your body there are other systems that form your Frequency Technology.

- The Spine is an antenna that receives cosmic Frequencies in waves.
- The Sacral at the base of the Spine contains 33 portals that run Frequencies all over your body.
- The Heart hosts your Life Force (held within a Sphere) which broadcasts your Frequencies in waves.

- The Brain decodes cosmic and localized Frequencies in waves and translates them into forms you can understand.
- Human DNA contains codes and data that interact with all Frequencies.

Your DNA uses two interlocking waves (the double helix) to interact with all other Frequencies.

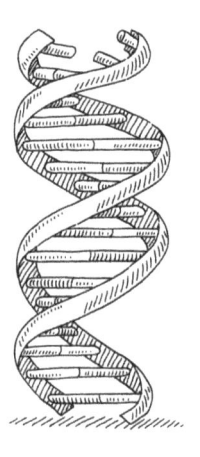

Diagram 3: DNA double helix.

Look at diagram 3. Observe two spirals connected like a ladder. Imagine that one spiral flows up, and one spiral flows down.

Wave 1 = spiral down pertains to your physical human nature. It is connected to your genetic heritage, ancestral experiences, etc.

Wave 2 = spiral up is connected to your nonphysical eternal nature. It links to who you are outside of Space Time.

These two waves literally vibrate you into form. When they are connected coherently they enable a human to have a multi-dimensional life experience, because they support an awareness that exists beyond the five senses.

Your human technology is grounded in the Earth's magnetic core, through her heart, via your body. This is why human coherence is so dependent upon the Earth. But your Frequencies broadcast beyond the Earth's electromagnetic field. They broadcast everywhere, all over the cosmos.

Everything affects us.
We affect everything.

Humans are complicated organisms. This is why we do not all resonate in the same way. Take a look around. People are having all kinds of experiences, vastly different and on the same planet. This has everything to do with Frequencies, and how we run them through our human body.

Frequencies create waves.
Waves create form.
Form is the environment we find ourselves in.

Your human body is a gift and an opportunity to impact your world. This is why ascended masters descend into a human body.

You are not what you think.

The Waves and Your Body

Part 2: Celestial

If you could spiritually x-ray yourself you would see a crystalline structure of luminous Golden Filaments. These resonate within an ocean of Holy Waters that flow in waves, and at your center you would observe an Eternal Flame. Your Life Force. God's Light.

Your body is a divinely organized structure.
Let that sink in.

At birth, a human teems with energy. Everything is dynamic and vital. Over time the body becomes burdened through a lack of understanding. The Frequency systems become blocked and the Life Force is stymied. People and oppressive or mundane routines can sap away at our Life Force. Toxic foods and living environments create low-Frequencies that slow down our natural systems leading to disease and decrepit old age.

That isn't how it was meant to be.

Humans simply forgot how our wondrous human technology works. Every so-called "empty space" or strand of "junk

DNA" or "spare" organ is a space that holds purpose. Your body contains a divine blueprint that is connected to all other divine blueprints. Everything is connected to everything and co-exists in the ever-present Now.

We call this connection element: The Golden Filaments.

The Golden Filaments permeate the physical cosmos and far beyond. It is a material that has not yet been fully understood. Neither fluid or gas, but something more resembling plasma, it moves in waves.

These are the Holy Waters of God. These are the creation elements. You could visualize The Golden Filaments as latticed snowflakes. Each one is elegantly different. Yet each one when connected renders a massive network of consciousness.

Collectively this network of Golden Filaments forms the mind of the Creator.

In school you were probably taught that you were no more than an intelligent ape. That you were the equivalent of a fruit fly in the vast expanse of time. Here today, gone tomorrow.

This is not true.

The human body is a divine technology of the Highest Order. This truth has been forgotten and even hijacked for numerous nefarious reasons. But this information was never truly lost. It is coded within our DNA. It is embedded in our Frequencies. It flows in our waves. We are in a time of remembering.

Order - which is Harmonic Resonance - is as intrinsic in the cosmos, as it is in the human body.

As Steven Strogatz noted in his work, *Sync:* How Order Emerges From Chaos in the Universe, Nature and Daily Life:

> "At the heart of the universe is a steady, insistent beat: the sound of cycles in sync …. These feats of synchrony occur spontaneously, almost as if nature has an eerie yearning for order."

Creator uses Harmonic Resonance, The Golden Filaments, and Holy Waters for evolutionary purposes. Order, resonance, and connectivity are at the heart of this process. Coherent Frequency waves produce more complex systems.

Ordered systems are more efficient. They have greater stability, functionality, abilities. This allows information and energy to transfer faster. Coherence is at the heart of The Waves, because this is a time of enormous evolutionary growth.

Our ability as humans to contemplate our role in the cosmos sets us apart from all living creatures on Earth. There is a natural yearning to reconnect to those greater, unseen and unknown aspects of ourselves. Through The Waves it is possible to enter these hidden realms through our human body, which we term Avatar.

There is a greater version of you that dwells outside of Space Time. In many Faith traditions this has been called either your Spirit* or your Soul. We prefer to use non-religious language when we refer to this grander aspect of ourselves. We use the word Fractal in place of the word Spirit. As this better represents the concept.

The word Spirit will be referred to throughout this book as Fractal.

Your Soul is not the same as your Fractal. It is not the same as your Avatar. Your Soul is an inter/multidimensional, sentient system that connects your Fractal to you as a human Avatar. The Soul is both localized and non-localized. Both here in our reality and elsewhere.

Your Soul resonates at a higher bandwidth than your electromagnetic field, accessing information inter/multidimensionally, yet it is capable of extending deeply into the third-dimension. In a sense then, our Soul is a vital, versatile feature of creation. It is no minor player.

Your Soul is integrated and coded into your DNA through your Avatar-blueprint. A single Soul can hold innumerable lifetimes, and innumerable human Avatars at a time. In fact, you reside simultaneously to the you-Now in innumerable renditions. This means that, theoretically, you could expand your consciousness into more than a single lifetime.

However, this lifetime, right Now, is the key.

This is because you chose this life to expand out from. It is also an auspicious time. So you're in the right body at the right time. This is an auspicious time for humanity. It is an opportunity to quantum-leap in evolutionary terms.

Everything you need to do this, is inside of your body.

Contemplation and Journal Section

What Teachings Resonated With Me in This Section?
Why?
How Does This Affect Me?

The Waves and the Cosmos

This chapter at a glance:

- Humans: Electromagnetic Fields, their Waves, Group Fields, Pulses, International Fields.

- The Earth's Electromagnetic Field, Nature's Fields, Planetary Resonance, Grids, Rods, Cones, Energy Lines, and Space Time.

- Cosmic: Waves, 26,000 Wave Pulse, Zero Point, and the nourishing Void.

The Waves and the Cosmos

In our previous chapters we discussed how Frequencies create waves, and how waves create realities. We explored how humans are made of waves and that these waves signal and receive information through their electromagnetic fields. We explored how the human body uses a Frequency wave technology we call The Waves. And that the heart, spine, sacrum, brain and DNA all interact with Frequency waves.

We learned that the totality of our waves generates our environment which in turn creates our life experiences.

Why are humans structured this way?

Simply put, it's in the blueprint. More elegantly put, it's because humans are made in the image of God, as many holy books declare. Technically we are a fractal of a Fractal of God. Kaya Usher describes humans as "godlings," co-creators in the making.

Everything about the human design has a multifaceted purpose. Electromagnetic fields are more than broadcast and magnetic centers. They generate and receive pulses.

Without a pulse, blood coagulates. Without the pulse of a current, water becomes stagnant. Without an electronic pulse, electricity would stop flowing. So too, there is a pulse that keeps all things in creation alive. That pulse comes from Zero Point at the heart of the multiverse.

It is the heart of God.

Pulses also carry an organism's blueprint codes. Every pulse reloads or refreshes the blueprint of that organism. Without the function of a pulse everything would come to a standstill and atrophy.

Everything pulses.

Pulses carry an electro-alchemical-magnetic charge. When a man and woman create a new human, the father's Life Force pulses the womb space into activation, and ignites fertilization. You felt your mother's Life Force pulse in the womb before you heard her heartbeat. Her pulse ignited your human body into animation. You are the offspring of co-creators. You were pulsed into being.

All humans pulse.

That is, they transmit a unique vibration that marks their Life Force out from all others. We resonate with life within a vast Frequency network. We impact and are impacted.

A pulse is not the same as a wave. It is the Life Force of a being, and it comes directly from the Creator, from Source. It is a sacred element that sustains everything. We can catch a glimpse of it when we observe a person glowing.

It's a beautiful radiance, a light that beams out of a healthy human.

A trace of it can be captured by Kirlian photography which captures the light from an individual's corona discharge. But it's more than the electrified magnetized air around them. It's a person's divine essence. At the center of this human aurora borealis dwells a brilliant golden light. This is your Life Force and it is beautiful.

If everything and everyone pulses and emanates waves, this implies that those closest to us would impact us more powerfully than those not. In fact, our primary relationships are highly magnetized.

Families are unified electromagnetic fields. Two people who come together create a Frequency resonance. Their electromagnetic fields become entangled. This is why the family is a powerful magnetic unit.

There are differences in how we resonate Frequency waves with others. There are those who are connected to us by blood. There are those who are connected to us through choice or circumstances. The former creates a deeper, unconscious and longer resonance field. The latter carries a lighter, faster and shorter resonance field. Both contribute to our human experience but they serve different functions.

Everyone on Earth impacts us somehow. Our planet is one giant network of human Frequencies: families, clans, friendship circles, co-workers, acquaintances, social groups, faith movements, political parties, and nation states.

Frequency resonance discernment is a subtle skill that comes with practice. Although in the beginning, it is often through trial and error, and eventually we can become an attuned and conscious observer.

Discernment is needed because while the higher Frequencies override the lower Frequencies, Group (or family) Frequencies are magnetic. If the gravitational magnetism of a Group (or family) is powerful enough, it will pull down a person's Frequencies like a corkscrew into waves of lower Frequency behaviors, attitudes, and actions. It takes time but it will happen.

The reason is that our human body is an electric-magnetic structure. Our electromagnetic field is magnetic. Gravity and Space Time affect it. Time, while linear, is actually circular, uncoiling like a spiral. Time is malleable.

For example, the outer coil in our first year of life feels like a century to an infant. The second coil, our toddler years, feels like decades. Remember how a school summer holiday seemed to go on and on? In reality it was just weeks that we took off from school. As we age the Time coil tightens and contracts, until in the end, years seem to fly by like hours. And they do.

Time is held within Space in the third-dimension and is magnetized. Space contains gravity which all beings experience. Although not as a fixed set of Newtonian laws. Matter is more fluid than solid. And Time is more elastic than fixed. So too, Gravity swirls and flows like a river depending on the Frequencies (waves) generated. In turn, waves are impacted by consciousness.

The elements of Space, Time and Gravity are influenced by the Frequencies of a Group (or family) creating pockets that can spiral us up or down. Discernment around Groups (and one's family) is therefore strongly advised.

It is equally true that a single person of a high resonance, can shift an entire nation. We can think of a person like Doctor Martin Luthor King Jr. or Joan of Arc. The point here is that we use discernment.

Frequency wave entanglement also occurs between teachers and students.

Teachers are beneficial for spurts of focused growth. They can entrain us into the higher Frequencies, simply by us being in their presence. Such individuals have their place, their rightful role. Eventually, however, we must become our own captains.

The Simplicity Platform's sixth Tenet: Sustain Our Frequency, is a powerful principle. If each of us contains God's Eternal Flame, then we are all holy vessels. We are responsible for our own evolution.

Teachers come in all guises. Some appear as the consequence of a troublesome relationship. There is wisdom in resonating for a time in friction. This means that there will be people, places, and experiences that we (choose to) magnetize to offer us specific lessons.

In fact, adversaries can be our greatest teachers. They offer us the opportunity to pivot quickly, to grow under pressure. They raise a mirror to the most unconscious aspects of ourselves. The key is reaching the epiphany moment and then releasing that teacher. There is no reason to prolong negative associations. We can allow experiences, and teachers of all kinds, to flow in and flow out as required.

Humanity is in the midst of a great evolutionary shift. In the electromagnetic fields of many, many beings there is a magnetic upswing.

> "Humanity is moving from individuation into unity. As a species humans learn through cyclical epochs, that is, vast expanses of linear Space Time. There are arcs and troughs that have pulled us into various frequency paradigms. The collective consciousness is coming back into prominence within Earth's localized frequency field.
>
> A new awareness is being ushered in. It is an understanding that we are all fractals of one another. We volunteered to come into physical form with one another (billions of us) to hold up a mirror to our blind spots. When we come into an expanded consciousness we appreciate the honor of co-existence, the wisdom of being triggered."
> Kaya Usher Free To Be 365.

We can all feel the shift from individual consciousness to global consciousness. Old hierarchies, top down power structures are ending. People are finding themselves moving into larger resonance fields that have a magnetism toward freedom, transparency and equality.

These are higher Frequencies.

Over time, the size of these movements will increase. They will build stronger fields that will flip the old reality, like a pancake and in the blink of an eye everything will change. That time has come.

It has everything to do with the Earth.

The Earth's electromagnetic field hosts other fields. These are fields resonating within nature. These are numerous, and diverse. Each field has its own self-organizing features and blueprints. For example, there is a localized field for trees and contained within it are the codes for an infinite variety of tree forms.

Harmonic Resonance is the velocity of the Earth's Frequency field, combined with the gravitational pull of her electromagnetic field as it spins in Space Time. She pulses a Life Force that sustains everything within her fields.

The Earth's Sphere is spinning faster. Her pulse is fanning higher Frequencies in waves. These waves are entraining everything on Earth. They are activating you. It is why you are here. If you have a stable Frequency velocity and a clear electromagnetic field, you will be able to absorb the Earth's pulse. You will be able to hold her evolutionary waves.

This is why you chose to incarnate at this time. It is significant because if enough humans stay in sync, Earth will ascend to a higher timeline. In other words, we can all build velocity and literally resonate in a new reality for our species.

How can the Earth ascend? A planet is a sentient being of a higher complexity than a human.

Her electromagnetic field resembles a grid of Golden Filaments. This grid is conscious and illuminated. This grid resonates within the greater Frequency Network.

Earth is a magnificent, beautiful, gracious being.

Take a few minutes to feel her brilliance.

The Earth is a magnified version of a human. She has many of the elements we have. For example, she possesses cones and rods. In the human eye, cones are the receptors responsible for sight. They convert the light that enters our eye into images and forms that we recognize.

The Earth uses cones within her grid to decode light into waves, creating a spectrum of holographic realities. We experience those realities as our life experiences. This is the reason why we have so many environments that humans can inhabit today.

The Earth offers us evolutionary pathways through these coexisting holographic realities. Your Fractal* yearns to know itself more deeply, a desire that is embedded within us from birth. Think about how you discovered what you're made of? More often than not, you learned through life experiences.

*Fractal = Spirit.

Our Fractal does the same. Your life came with a preloaded set of challenges, conditions and interactions with others.

Then, you descended into a Frequency-generated reality specifically hosted by our Earth.

That's how powerful you are.

Let's go a little deeper. If the Earth's cones act as simulators of holographic realities, her rods act as Frequency devices. These rods vibrate beneath the Earth's grid and are rooted into the Earth's Ley Lines*.

*Highly magnetized energy meridian lines.

These rods hold information in the form of holographic plates*. These plates are located all over the globe.

*Holographic plates are localized fields of information.

Our DNA acts like a key. We can access the information held within these plates based upon it. This is why sages traveled along certain routes. The paths they walked were often aligned with Ley Lines, and connected to powerful vortex centers. But they also took these routes to tap into the information contained within the holographic plates located there. This augmented their own illumination.

Great teachers walked these routes for three primary reasons: to visit auspicious energy sites and gain more illumination, to share their wisdom with others along the way and to connect to their other lifetimes, their other Avatars via the holographic plates.

We can think of it as leaving a note in a bottle for ourselves and tossing that bottle into the ocean of Space Time. Or as leaving our future selves a Frequency time capsule within the Earth's grid.

Why would we do this? We would do it to release previously lost and forgotten information, and to harness more Frequencies.

When a life of significance is lived, it resonates within a locality. It leaves a mark. An aware human can connect to many lives resonating across many lifetimes, with sometimes, thousands of years apart. Yet, with enough consciousness, a person can tap into those other versions of themselves. The point is Oneness, to come back into unification and to expand.

You can remember many lives and unlock many ages too. These abilities were known to the ancients and will be known again. The key is to become so expansive, and so aware *in this lifetime* that your consciousness begins to sense other versions of you. All living in a Point of Now* (P.O.N).

Your current present moment.

An example would be a particularly enlightened 16th century version of you living in their P.O.N, which is simultaneous to your current P.O.N. Now is the eternal moment, the Golden Mean that connects every single Now-moment. Consciousness closes the gap.

We can illustrate how consciousness can collapse Space Time and connect two P.O.Ns centuries apart.

Take a sheet of paper. Mark an A near the top of the page and a B near the bottom of the page.

A = your life now

B = your life in the 16th Century

There are a few ways to get from A to B. One way is to go down the page from A to B, which for our purposes would be a passage of time of 400 years. This would involve a few incarnations, deaths, births, etc.

A more efficient way would be to fold the page down the middle, *to fold Space Time,* thus overlapping A and B allowing you to circumvent 400 years into one single mark or P.O.N.

How can we connect with our other selves?

Our Fractal will always give us clues. It might begin with a fascination for a particular time period and place. You might watch an historical movie or read a book about a location that feels familiar to you. Maybe you'll have vivid recurring dreams about another time period. Those are the breadcrumb trails for you to follow.

Remember, this information can feel ethereal or subtle when it first begins to bleed through the veil. From the perspective of your Fractal, and through your Soul, you are already cognizant of your other lifetimes.

As we've stated, memories can be triggered along the Earth's energy lines. In fact, many people experience deja vu and a sense of familiarity when they travel. This is because you have entered a field where another version of you is living. Their life and experience is held for you in a holographic plate. You are co-existing in the same Space, but not the same Time.

However, as we showed with the folded paper, we can instigate an overlap. If this happens to you, be still and try to clear your mind. This isn't something to force. Feelings and emotions may come up for you. The information is stored in holographic plates and if there is something for you to bring into your consciousness, it will be released to you.

Space Time is a construct. A map that our Fractal uses to track its journeys through many renditions and lifetimes. In conjunction with gravity and Ley Lines, Space Time offers us a holographic frame for self-reference.

Ley Lines hold a powerful current of energy that uses gravitational forces. They form a grid that holds the Earth in stability, and anchors all life to her core. Ley Lines can be harnessed for free energy. Our ancestors utilized their energy in the distant past. Ley Lines run through many sacred sites, which is not a coincidence. These sites can be used to charge and to ground our electromagnetic fields.

Ley Line energy is neutral and they have been leveraged for positive and negative intentions. Now, the Earth is bringing her Ley Lines back into balance.

The Earth, like other planets and galaxies, is affected by external forces. For example, every 26,000 years, a pulse resonates from the center of our multiverse. This is the Frequency equivalent of a tsunami. This 26,000 cosmic pulse sends waves that fan out everywhere.

These waves activate quantum leaps in evolution or great resets. We can think of this pulse as the Creator's heartbeat. Kaya Usher calls this Zero Point. We are living in such a time. The 26,000 pulse has sent waves that have reached us here on Earth.

We too possess an ability to reset, to pulse using Zero Point. When we surrender and let go we find ourselves embodied in the present-moment. This automatically expands our consciousness, our waves pulse higher Frequencies. This is Zero Point. This is Free Fall.

Zero Point is the source of all creation and a portal into the greatest of Holy Mysteries. A place that existed before all creation, before Space Time, and even before God.

Contemplation and Journal section

What Teachings Resonated With Me in This Section?
Why?
How Does This Affect Me?

Activation: Grounding Golden Sovereign Technique

We close out each Section of The Waves with a technique called Grounding Golden Sovereign Technique.

This technique will not only connect you to the Earth's magnetic core it will also connect you more deeply into your own golden filament system. Your Golden Filaments system acts like a network that connects your Frequencies, literally your Life Force, to your organic, flesh and blood human body.

This first Section of The Waves, called Emergence has closed. It is time to go within and assimilate what we have learned. The following technique is designed to help you integrate Emergence. We recommend that you record your own voice speaking these words as this will help to entrain your mind more deeply.

(CLOSING ACTIVATION)

Find a comfortable quiet place to sit or lay down.
Turn off all of your gadgets or mute them.
Touch or hold your natural object (stone, feather, cone, etc).
If it is a candle, gently watch the flickering flame.
Take a few deep breaths in and get comfortable.

You are going to bring your awareness back into your body first through feeling your breath in, breath out.

Breathe in
Breathe out

Breathe in
Breathe out

Breathe in
Breathe out

Breathe in
Breathe out

Feel that breath of life as it is taken around your body.

Feel your Life Force as it meanders around what looks like a network that runs all over your body, from the top of your head to the tips of your toes.

It looks like the other systems in your body: the capillary, the lymph, artery systems and yet this network is so vibrant, so powerful, it is luminous.

This is your Frequency network.

Everything is interconnected. Feel your Life Force moving around your Frequency network, lighting it up, aglow. Feel the warmth of that Life Force, warmed by your Eternal Flame.

In your head count down from 33 to 20.

33 32 31 30 29 28 27 26 25 24 23 22 21 20

Deeper and deeper journey through your Frequency network, feeling every single part of your body resonating as one unified system.

Feel that.

In your head count down from 19 to 10.

19 18 17 16 15 14 13 12 11 10

Feel your own resonance.

In your head count down from 9 to zero.

9 8 7 6 5 4 3 2 1 Zero

See yourself as a Frequency Light Being, generating a dazzling light that beams out to form a golden electromagnetic field. Feel that.

You see a giant, glowing ball in the distance.

Is it the sun?
No, it is our Earth.

You are seeing her as a Frequency Being.

She is radiant, luminous.
She glows within a brilliant gridwork of light.
The Frequency field she projects is enormous.
It feels warm.
It feels inviting.
You can hear a faint pulse like a heartbeat.
With each pulse the grid is lit up.
In between the pulse it glows a little softer.

There's a magnetic pull.
It feels like love.
Now, move towards her.
Feel her warmth.
Feel her light.

You enter her electromagnetic field.
You stop at her center.
It feels like a warm blanket, a burrow to curl up in.
Even though her electromagnetic field is bright, here.
Here, it is dark and soothing.
It smells like the hearth, of soft soil, of wood, of rain.

Stretch out your arms and legs and touch the luminous lines you feel all about you.
Feel our Earth connect to your Frequency network.
Feel that surge of Frequencies.
It lights you up.
It fills your body.
And yet, you are held in the comforting darkness of her core.
The gentle beat of her heart.

Boom Boom Boom Boom
Boom Boom Boom Boom
Boom Boom Boom Boom

Boom Boom Boom Boom

Safe - connected - activated - grounded.

Feel that.

(Fall gently into silence for 21 seconds)

21 20 19 18 17 16 15 14 13 12 11 10 9 8 7 6 5 4 3 2 1 zero

Feel that.

Take that with you always.

INTEGRATION

We recommend that you take at least one week away from this book and just be.

Reflections on Emergence

Ponder on the following or create some concepts from Section 1 in the following notes section.

"A state of profound self-awareness and observation of previously obscured or hidden elements that require release or integration. These elements arise from our subconscious and the Spheres, where humans normally have limited access."
What has come up for you lately?

"Be as solid as a rock, as light as a feather."
What does this mean to you?

"Frequencies vibrate in waves. We come to resonate this path *in Waves.*"
How does this make you feel?

"We came here to resonate waves and shift reality. It's not the other way around."
How do you feel about this?

While reading this book, spend as much time as you can in nature. What Frequency partners (inanimate objects) have you chosen? They can be a feather, a stone, a pebble, a pine cone, a shell, a plant or a beeswax candle. As many things as you wish to collect. Have them with you when you read this book.
How do these partners resonate with you?

Practice Ideas:

- Become aware of any differences in sensations, energy flow, even pain, in your body.
- Practice grounding techniques. (Barefoot on grass, being in nature, grounding shoes, etc)
- Connect to your Frequency partners (inanimate object/s) and ask for their guidance.
- Journal or reflect upon your experiences, feelings and dreams.

Contemplation and Journal section

Emergence Notes:

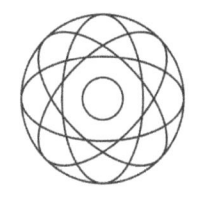

Section 2

Osmosis

"A state of reconnection to previously hidden or blocked elements. This is a feeling space. We feel first through our heart and our bodies and then we process through our headspace. This can sometimes be challenging and uncomfortable. We absorb what is useful and we release what is not. Osmosis is a holistic process." Kaya Usher The Waves course.

Section 2: Osmosis

Contents:

- Harmonic Resonance.
- Blueprint vs Imprint.
- Free Fall.
- Imprints and Family.
- Fractal, Soul, Avatar.
- The Three Spheres.
- The Principles: Avatar Mechanics.
- Grounding Golden Sovereign Technique.

Activation: Harmonic Resonance

We always begin with Harmonic Resonance.

Settle down.
Get comfortable.
I invite you to count out loud.

Count down from 21 to zero.
Follow your breath.
Feel your body.

21 20 19 18 17 16 15 14 13 12 11
10 9 8 7 6 5 4 3 2 1 Zero

You are going to open up an activation space.

- Golden Filaments
- Holy Waters
- Sphere
- Electromagnetic field

Count down from 33 to Zero silent in your mind.

33 32 31 30 29 28 27 26 25 24 23 22 21
20 19 18 17 16 15 14 13 12 11
10 9 8 7 6 5 4 3 2 1 0

Free Fall into yourself.
Hear these words and activate.
Sphere.

Velocity.
Magnetism.
Spin.
Light.

Harmonic Resonance.
Hum "AUM" aloud.

AUM
AUM
AUM
AUM
AUM
AUM
AUM
AUM
AUM

Fall into silence for as long as you are called to.

Blueprint vs Imprint

This chapter at a glance:

- Your Blueprint, blueprint.
- Your Imprints.

Blueprint vs Imprint

The Waves technology has now emerged.
What does that mean?

It means that the work you have decided to do is here. Everything has been done by You. You called this book into your field. In reading what we have written, you have come into communion with it. Our time together in the space of this book is just that.

A collaboration.

We always call to mind Tenet 5 of The Simplicity Platform:

> "Ours is not a space for rules, dogma or gurus. Ours is an Independence space."

We take this seriously. We honor your own journey with this material. With each page you turn you will come in more fully. You will be called to stretch your wings, to lean in and to build your own velocity. Our role is simply to facilitate that. We hold a space with you.

In Section 1, we experienced an Emergence of The Waves. Emergence comes as an exploration of ideas. Together we explored:

- How Frequencies create waves and how waves create matter.
- How humans are made of waves and that we signal and receive waves through our electromagnetic field.
- How our waves generate our environment which in turn creates our life experiences.
- How each human experiences reality differently because of this.
- How other electromagnetic fields affect us. These are things like family fields, group fields, nature's fields and the Earth's electromagnetic field.
- How the Earth's Rods, Cones, and Ley Lines impact us.
- How Space Time, gravity, cosmic waves, Zero Point and the 26,000 pulse deeply affect all beings.

We open our minds to these concepts and let them sit. We needn't dwell too much on them unless we are called to. Integration of The Waves occurs naturally through-out the process of reading this book, by joining like-minded others, through being in solitude, and through immersion in nature.

Everything in life is an integration.

Osmosis is the next stage of the process. This is when The Waves are heard within us, received back and forth through a gentle oscillation of inner communion. This is when they will bubble up and surface as expressions, feelings, thoughts and emotions. Your Frequencies do the work. All you need to do is let go.

This is Free Fall.

From here on we move into Osmosis. Imagine the sounds of waves gently crashing to the shore and read these words aloud:

Osmosis of The Waves, once set in motion, is continuous.
Once experienced, Osmosis of The Waves is a process of embodiment.
Once encountered, Osmosis of The Waves is a journey of great expansion.
Osmosis of The Waves is an endeavor that points the way towards Transfiguration.
Osmosis is about who I AM fundamentally.
(Take a pause)

What is this I AM?

It is You as a Fractal with its own God-given Blueprint, aglow and shimmering. Just like a fingerprint, it is unique and one of a kind.

Then, it is you as part of a Soul.
It is you as an awake Avatar.

Feel that.

What is a Blueprint?
A Blueprint is the Fractal's original setting.

The Creator gives each Fractal its Blueprint upon its inception. This is more than a Frequency ID. A Fractal's Blueprint holds all of its potentiality in limitless expression. In other words, it doesn't lock a Fractal in, into a programmed destiny.

A Fractal's Blueprint also holds its connection to Source yet it sets it completely free to journey and to experience and to express. It is Home and is unchangeable, and yet it is also dynamic and holds all possibilities. It is the start of every journey.

Once we move outside of Space Time a paradox like this makes total sense.

A Fractal's Blueprint is the terminal through which ...
all and every purpose
all and every experience
all and every rendition
all and every dimension
all and every environment
... is filtered through.

Your Fractal's Blueprint is unknowable and yet, it is the most familiar aspect of who you are. A paradox that is Truth.

It is ...
untouchable
incorruptible
unfathomable
... feel that.

Your Fractal is made in the image of God. Therefore, you are made in God's image. Your divine nature exists outside of Space Time and is infinite.

All Fractals emerged within God *almost* identical to one another, and contains an aspect of the others like a prism.

A Fractal's evolution is the consequence of its desire to individuate. Individuation comes from taking a journey (an infinite amount of journeys) laden with experiences, with challenges and surprises within a generated environment.

Each journey has its own purpose. It may be some aspect of ascension (remembering, expanding) or some aspect of descension (forgetting, contraction: Free Falling within). It can be everything in-between. Some journeys are even run on autopilot. Everything is available to a Fractal.

Fractals pursue Self-Awareness while knowing that All are One.

So, you are a part of something beyond your wildest comprehension. The purpose of your particular life (Now) sustains you, is you, and is contained within your individual blueprint.

That's your I AM.

Avatar-blueprint

Every human Avatar has its own unique blueprint*. It holds the purpose of your life. It is who you are at your core underneath all the layers. It is coded with all of your potential. It contains everything that you need to evolve.

Avatar-blueprint is our individual blueprint, and is given to us by our Fractal. Fractal-Blueprint refers to our Fractal, and is given to it by God at its inception.

Osmosis is an integration of you into your Avatar-blueprint.

This is embodiment.

Avatar-blueprints vs Imprints
Your Avatar-blueprint is not the same as your imprint/s. An imprint is the process of adding layers of experience (integration) to your blueprint. It's an experience stamp within Space Time.

These have enormous value for our Fractal.

A significant human Avatar life leaves a mark upon a Fractal. These are then imprinted over a Fractal's Blueprint. This is how a Fractal evolves. Each imprint adds more value in terms of self-awareness, self-determination and individuation.

In summary, your Fractal can access all of your experiences as imprints (within third-dimensional Space Time) held within your blueprint. The most significant imprints are extracted and added to a Fractal's Blueprint.

Can you see how important you are in this process?

Contemplation and Journal section

What Teachings Resonated With Me in This Section?
Why?
How Does This Affect Me?

Free Fall

This chapter at a glance:

- The IF poem.
- Free Fall and the Fall of Humanity.
- To Fall with Child.

Free Fall

When a Fractal chooses to descend in order to individuate, it utilizes a technique called Free Fall. We have mentioned this before and now we will expand upon it.

Individuation involves loss, pain, suffering and separation as much as it involves joy, love, epiphany and union. This is why we speak of Free Fall throughout this book. Free Fall makes living in a Free Will Zone easier, because it is a complete surrender, the letting go of all attachment to outcome. Resistance creates friction, interference within Frequency fields. This causes internal turbulence. Free Fall overrides this.

Free Fall is not an easy thing to do, let alone practice but it holds the key to everything.

Free Fall is something for you to focus on now, as it is an important stage of Osmosis. Free Fall does not require that you give anything of yourself away in order to reach enlightenment. So separate letting go of all attachments to sacrifice. They are not the same things. When we Free Fall we enter into Zero Point, where everything exists in potentiality.

This is the equivalent of pulling up the oars of our canoe and flowing into a waterfall, as opposed to paddling furiously upstream away from it.

How can you practice Free Fall?

Below is a poem that you can use to let go. You can edit and make this poem your own. Insert elements of your life that hold weight or power over you. It can be a person or persons, places and things. You could create a set of mindful cards to keep bringing you back into a state of Free Fall.

Note the feelings that arise from these statements. What resistance is triggered? How does your body feel? Observe. Feel. Everything.

IF

If nothing changed for me ever
Would it be enough?

If everyone left me tomorrow
Would I be enough?

If this room were all I had
Would it be enough?

If this moment were all I had
Would it be enough?

If this life were all I had.
Would it be enough?

If nothing else at all existed but me.
Would it be enough?

Use this poem when you feel especially stuck or overcome with "wants" or "distractions" or "people" and when you feel dissatisfied with your life. These are all attachments.

Saying these words aloud will initiate a deep release. As you say the words out loud, feel everything and then let it go.

The point of each statement in the poem is to strip you back to your Avatar-blueprint. It is designed to flag up attachments and resistance. These statements may feel frightening. The thought of being utterly alone, or of being confined to one life or to a single room is uncomfortable. Yet, underneath each and every uncomfortable feeling is a Truth.

You are enough.

The world's merchants and rulers want us to reach outside of ourselves, so we are constantly bombarded with desires, wants, dreams and everyone of them comes with an attachment. A payload that is temporary and leaves a weight that pulls us down into the lower-Frequencies.

Attachments also create voids within us, causing us to feel "less than" and empty. We hear the sirens of consumerism, the hawks of materialism calling "this will fill you." It never does, like junk food it offers a temporary fix but leaves us hungrier. On and on it goes, an endless consumption of stuff. A hamster wheel of desire.

Another obstacle to Free Fall is resistance. Resistance produces interference in the flow of life, like static on a radio station. Resistance comes in many forms. Ego-based, it arises from a need to control things, and stay in the familiar. It involves dismissing synchronicities and ignoring opportunities because they terrify us, or lead to unknowable outcomes. Resistance is a refusal to see something that isn't working in our lives. It's avoidance.

When we practice Free Fall we give up all resistance to life. We step away from our programs, our need to control everything. Free Fall takes practice and patience. Here are some steps to aid detachment.

1. Observe your attachments: habits, people, places, things, without judgment.
2. Observe your resistance: avoidance, ignoring, refusal to see.
3. Notice the weight behind these things.
4. Let go. Free Fall.
5. (Say aloud) "I let go of all attachments to X, Y, Z."
6. Pause. Blank. Stillness.
7. Let go. Free Fall.
8. (Say aloud) "I let go of all resistance to A, B, C."
9. Pause. Blank. Stillness.
10. Feel your body (lightness).
11. Say aloud: "And so it is."
12. Ground yourself.

Your body is your greatest teacher. It will keep you grounded as you let go. Ungrounded detachment can feel cold, unloving. When we release without attachment we move from conditional love into unconditional love. This is because we resonate with others and with things without attachment. We do not need nor desire them in of themselves, which means we love and live freely. Others will feel this freedom.

Loving without attachment because the One is Enough. Loving this way frees you up to love Everything.

You are complete. A Holy creation. A godling, luminous, radiant, and brilliant.

Hear this Truth.

Your Life is an act of veneration. Your heart is the mediator. God does not seek nor need worship, or obedience. Creator seeks communion through resonance. There are no rituals or orders to access this relationship. You do not have to sacrifice anything to experience it. Creator loves without attachment, without expectation, and without desire.

That's Free Fall.

You are only invited to walk in joy, to be as light as a feather (a clear electromagnetic field) and to be as solid as a rock (grounded to our Earth). Which means you hold onto nothing (for you need nothing). You are all things. Free Fall means forgiveness which is letting go of yourself and all others.

Free Fall may at times feel like a death.

This is because letting go of people, places and things is an act of dying. Letting go of resistance can be frightening. You may experience periods of blankness. You may have a sensation of being adrift. It can feel as though a rug was pulled from under your feet.

That is entirely normal. Stay with it. This practice of Free Fall requires perseverance. Grounding techniques like earthing (bare foot) and meditating will help to keep you balanced. Nature will always be there for you. Kaya Usher's Grounding Golden Sovereign Technique that tethers us to the Earth was developed precisely for this purpose.

During this practice of Free Fall expect miracles, anticipate serendipities. Go with your flow. Give everything you knew up. Try something different. Take a different route to work, for example. Act on your intuition. Say yes to an opportunity even if it frightens you. Yes represents alignment, attunement. Say "yes" when it feels right. When it resonates as right.

Free Fall and The Fall of Humanity

> "The more we fall the more momentum we gain. This technology builds and builds its charge which allows us to expand ad infinitum. This is the true meaning of the term "The Fall of Man." It has been inverted and corrupted through millennia. The more we let go the more momentum we pick up."
> Kaya Usher Free To Be 365.

The "Fall of Humanity" as depicted in many holy texts is misleading. When the two human archetypes Eve and Adam chose to push outside of their blissful paradise and asked "what else is there?" they were surrendering to the unknown, the unknowable.

Independence through questing comes with challenges that force evolution. Adam and Eve had to make a life outside of their prison paradise. A choice that wasn't without real hardships. But in return they achieved sovereignty and eventually laid the path towards enlightenment for the human race.

Their quest began by leaving the familiar, comforting support system of Eden. That was an enormous loss that was given in exchange for the freedom to self-determine, to travel, and create societies. By doing so, Eve and Adam were reenacting the desire of the One that had left the eternal bliss of the nourishing Void. This One is the great Something, the First Cause, Creator God.

To Fall with Child

When a woman is said to have "fallen with child" this is a correct understanding of Free Fall. In the moment she conceives, a woman embodies the nourishing Void as the great Mother. The spark of fertilization initiated by the Father's role in procreation ignites a new life form in the primordial waters of the woman's uterus.

This is a God Space activation, a calling into being. This spark grows into the Eternal Flame manifesting a divine form in those dark waters. The child is a result of the mother's womb and her egg, and the ignition of fertilization by the father's sperm.

Eventually, the baby will be impelled to leave its safe watery home and enter into a world of unknowns. Over the course of a human life, it will quest, and risk, and Free Fall through innumerable experiences into self-realization.

To Fall is the same as Free Fall in that it is an action of surrender into the unknown without attachment. Kaya Usher calls this point of Free Fall Zero Point.

Free Fall is encoded in our DNA. It initiates separation from the known and movement towards the unknown. This is why young adults separate away from their family unit and quest. It is the reason why our ancient ancestors left familiar homelands and migrated across great plains of wilderness.

Humans are hard-wired to adventure, and to ask questions that appear to have no answer. We separate and Free Fall (surrender) because it's more than a choice. It's a deep yearning. An uncharted world offers us a pathway to self-realization.

This is Free Fall in the I AM space.

The Waves produce phenomena that aren't always easy to explain. But there is no secret, no great mystery. There is only Truth. And the Truth is always simple.

The Truth within You is Time Stamped. Meaning that only when you are ready, can you experience Truth. And you decide that for yourself. Free Fall is a powerful practice that is unique to you. There is no one above you, ahead of you, because there is no single "right" path. There are no elaborate rites of passage or initiations.

It's just you.
Blueprinted.
Imprinted.

Contemplation and Journal section

What Teachings Resonated With Me in This Section?
Why?
How Does This Affect Me?

Imprints and Family

This chapter at a glance:

- Your Family.
- Your Lineage, Bloodline.
- Your Lives: Present, Past, Future.
- Your Imprints and Space Time.

Imprints and Family

Our life unfolds through a series of experiences that imprint us.

What is an imprint?

We can visualize imprinting as a scribe patiently, and lovingly overlaying a manuscript's inked pages with gold, with cobalt blue, with royal red. A process that enhances the manuscript into illumination.

Your experiences are such embellishments.
Adornments. Embossments. Imprints.

Your human canvas hosts an infinite spectrum of expression, an inexhaustible Free Will, an innumerable spectrum of choices. Yours is not a "color between the lines" space.

Osmosis of the Waves is the practice of Synthesis. It's a renovation of a masterpiece without losing the luster of its age. It's all of the knowledge, all of the experiences filtered through wisdom and everything without any attachment.

This process takes discernment. Not all imprints are equal. Otherwise our imprints would simply accumulate, creating clutter, distortions and obscurity - like a bunch of scribbles over an etching.

Unconscious imprints are distortions disguised. They come from many sources. Our birth family being foremost.

The Simplicity Platform 8 Tenets was designed to Clean Up the family Space. This is why we continue to work the Tenets as a foundation practice while studying more complex Frequency Technologies. Osmosis of The Waves takes us a step further, a step wider and deeper.

As we shall learn, The Waves Osmosis permeates into …
our subconscious mind
our dreamscape
our bloodline
our innumerable lifetimes
… this is what makes it more potent.

Osmosis is an awareness of what is of us and what is not.

For example, before we reach a state of conscious awareness most of our imprinting is done by others. Imprints are passed down through our blood lineage, from one generation to another. These become the habits, traits, beliefs and opinions of our particular family that shape us.

All humans arise from a single family, which broke off into clans and tribes. Those tribes then broke off into separate ethnic groups based upon geography, dialect, weather, and diet. These ethnic groups took on imprints of culture, habits and beliefs. In turn, these variations broke off into a vast global network of families. But these differentials are cosmetic compared to what connects us as humans. We are one family, one bloodline.

Your bloodline carries the imprint of your ancestors. Their imprints came from their experiences. All lineages have experienced great challenges: famines, natural disasters, plagues, and wars. All bloodlines have experienced cycles of poverty, of scarcity, and of fear, over and over and over again.

Our ancestral experiences generate heavy, low-resonating Frequencies that are imprinted from parent to child. These imprints are Time Stamped. They create distortion patterns that run through each generation. This is what causes families to perpetuate the same habits, beliefs and experiences as their ancestors.

The consequence is a literal generation.

Each generation generates these imprints afresh solidifying them even further, making them more powerful, more magnetic. We might think of actors on a stage performing the same play, reading the same lines, and playing the same roles over and over again. This is why people often feel that their life runs on a loop. And if 95% of their time is lived unconsciously, that would be a correct understanding.

Life is meant to flow.
We were designed to break the mold.
Evolve or repeat.

If we don't evolve we repeat until we awaken. For this reason in every generation comes one or more who volunteer to act as a circuit-breaker. This person is a pioneer, a catalyst. They are often called "The Black Sheep" of the family and treated with bias. We prefer to call this person the Circuit Breaker.

In truth, the entire family agreed for the Circuit Breaker to come. Their role is to disrupt the unconscious imprints running through a bloodline. These individuals are so powerful they can stop unconscious imprinting passing into all future generations with just their one life. They do this a few ways:

- They confront the imprint.
- They refuse to run the imprint.
- They embody the pain behind it and release it.

They can also release all previous generations from unconscious lineage imprinting. This freedom reverberates like ripples on a lake. It touches everything.

Are you that person?

The Circuit Breaker often has a difficult time breaking free. Blood is iron-based, so our bloodlines are deeply magnetic and we choose them for what they can teach us, about ourselves, about others.

Consciousness gives us the ability to pull back and see our connection to all Earth bloodlines. That we are all One and yet free to be individuated. So, bloodlines have an incredible value. They offer us pathways for experiences across Space Time and much like a vacation, we get to choose:

Where we want to go on Earth.
What we want to experience.
Who we want to travel with.
What we want to bring home with us back into our Fractal's Blueprint.

How can you uncover valuable Imprints using The Waves?

Stay in the present moment.
Remain embodied (in your body).
Observe the imprints that are running continuously through your life without judgment.
Observe your loved ones.

Question everything, ask: is this *of me* or has it come from *someone else*?

Observe and offer no resistance. Resistance pushes these imprints more deeply into your unconscious mind. You want to simply watch your thoughts, your beliefs, your words, your habits as they arise.

Many families can literally hum with the fear vibration. Again, no judgment, we just observe. The truth is, we have no idea what our ancestors endured and survived in the distant past. Laying low and not moving against herd consensus likely preserved their lives. But we shouldn't let that family trait hold us back. Playing it safe to stay alive is not a useful survival strategy for us.

Risk and extreme trials are not to be avoided. We can think of Edith Eger. A woman who, as a young girl, was transported to Auchswitz in 1944.

In her book, *The Choice*, she writes:

> "The second step in the dance for freedom is learning how to take risks that are necessary to true-realization."

For Edith, risk is keenly connected to truth, to growth and to healing. This is why we push our way through negative experiences. It is a path to Self-Realization.

What about imprints of personal trauma? Traumas that stake you to a specific place in time? Traumas that continue to emit dense, heavy, slow-resonating Frequencies? A trauma that keeps looping in your pain even though many years have passed since it occurred?

This is common.

Trauma forms a magnetic field that pulls us back into the pain. And when a memory is triggered, our emotions reactivate the original trauma and imprint it more deeply. How can we shift that?

You can release yourself from the weight of trauma. Countless people have felt an enormous relief using Kaya Usher's Frequency Technologies. It is possible to recircuit, to release the charge behind a trauma and release it from our electromagnetic field. Once it's released, the trigger is removed and we are liberated from that moment in Space Time.

Edith Eger achieved this through the power of forgiveness which filled her with Grace (a high-Frequency) and transfigured her life from one of chronic suffering and victimhood into one of illumination and profound wisdom.

This is the embellishment that we spoke of earlier. You become an illuminated being, like the works in the Book of Kells*. You use your experiences, positive and negative, as powerful growth tools. This is spiritual alchemy, metaphysics.

*The Book of Kells is an illuminated manuscript created approximately 800 AD and on display in Trinity College in Dublin, Ireland.

Trauma release involves embodying the experience and pulling in every fragment of it into full consciousness. This doesn't mean we only run it through our headspace by talking about it. It must also be felt in our body. Emotions plus feelings plus sensations plus thoughts combined maintain a traumatic block within our electromagnetic field.

We understand that this isn't an easy thing to do. Bringing a trauma back into full consciousness often takes time. It is important to seek the appropriate support while you do this. You will need help in releasing the trauma from your body for example and there are many modalities and therapies available for that.

The point is to pull in every fragment of our trauma through Osmosis.

Traumas shatter us on every level and set down deep imprints. Imprints that we can pass down to our own descendents. The Waves is a technology that pulls everything that needs healing into view. It contains an innate wisdom.

This is Osmosis.

Dreams are another realm that we can access to pull up traumas. Everything can be used. For everyone, the Osmosis of trauma is different. It could take years. It could happen in a flash. Just bear in mind that once initiated, Osmosis will begin its deep search and retrieve operation. It will flush things out. So you will need to be patient, to be kind with yourself. You will need to ask for help at times.

Remember, the trauma doesn't actually define you. It is what comes from the trauma - growth, wisdom, self-realization - that is imprinted back into your blueprint. That's the value. Everything else (the person, the events, the time and place) you can purge and jettison.

Eventually, with time and practice you could clear every trauma from this lifetime and experience a greater state of coherence. We call this the Lightness of Being, and it is pure Brilliance. This is you choosing yourself.

> "It takes courage to decide to put your foot down and walk toward your natural state of being. When you decide to take this journey on, day in, day out, you enter into a covenant with your divine Self."
> Kaya Usher Free To Be 365.

This is the Power of The Waves *through* You.

There are many lost and traumatized aspects of yourself beyond this lifetime. Think about the countless lives you have lived, and the time periods lived in. The opportunities to have been imprinted through severe traumas is obvious.

These lives are not done and dusted, and archived away in the akashic records. All life resonates in the present-moment. Every life you have ever lived on Earth is happening right

Now. Your past lives, your present life, and all future lives are all occurring *in this present moment.*

You have been offered the choice to experience every conceivable human identity and culture through Osmosis. Relax your mind and allow it to think about different time periods. You have the ability to pull in every other part of yourself. Here, and on other planets and in other dimensions. All with the goal of deeper individuation.

This is the meaning of Illumination.
Everything is about Self-Realization.

The Waves

Contemplation and Journal section

What Teachings Resonated With Me in This Section?
Why?
How Does This Affect Me?

Cosmic Structure: Fractal, Soul and Avatar

This chapter at a glance:

- Fractal.
- Soul.
- Avatar.
- The Three Spheres: Awake life; Sleep time; In-between Spaces before Birth, after Death.

Fractal, Soul, Avatar

The Waves demystifies the human experience. There are three main components to creation: Fractal, Soul and Avatar. They all serve an integral function and are important.

God. Omniscient Creator, Prime Cause, the One who made all things dwells as the totality of these components.

1. Fractal / Spirit. Our true home, Blueprint and teacher.
2. Soul, an internal sentient system that a Fractal uses to manifest, manage Avatars.
3. Avatar, the human questing agent of a Fractal.

As God utilizes the process of fractalization to experience ITS all-knowing. Fractals utilize Souls to generate experiences. Souls birth human Avatars (and other renditions) as experience agents.

The Fractal

Diagram 4: A Fractal.

A Fractal is a unit of God. It is both God and an individuated aspect of God.

A Fractal offers Creator a specific reflection of ITS totality, like one cut of a diamond. There is an unknowable number of Fractals. They do not exist outside of God. Everything exists as God.

Creator seeks to know ITSELF in relation to knowing all things - as Source. This is because knowing all things without a context is the equivalent of knowing nothing. Without context, all-knowing exists as raw data, as theory, which is pure potentiality. Everything is an unrealized thought in the Mind of Creator until it is experienced within a context.

In order to experience an experience, there are three requirements:

1. The purpose for an experience.
2. The environment for an experience to occur.
3. The experience agent / mechanism.

Fractals offer Creator all three of the above. (1) Out of an infinite number of purposes, one is selected.

(2) A Fractal can localize an experience within an environment. Not all environments are hosted within Space Time. (3) Fractals generate experience mechanisms and agents: souls, avatars, other beings.

This isn't out-sourcing. It is in-sourcing. Source is all, therefore, all is Source. So the only action taken by Source is to in-source everything to its innumerable Fractals.

It's natural to view this Fractal structure as a system of compartmentalization. Only it isn't. Fractals are not *at one* with God. They *are* God. Fractals are divinely interconnected to everything in creation (to one another) and are also uniquely individuated.

Creator God is the omniscience, the omnipotence and the omnipresence of this Fractalized structure. IT is the consciousness ITSELF. IT is the Source of this system of creation. This is why so many adepts speak of the *Mind of God*.

Creator is the Source, the totality of all that is, will be, has been.

We could visualize this Divine consciousness as a vast ocean that contains an infinite spectrum of creatures. Each creature has its own movements, its own purpose, its own expression. These expressions impact the ocean, individually and collectively. Yet, they cannot be anything other than aspects of that ocean.

The ocean remains an ocean.
The ocean is.

Fractals represent vast shoals of marine life, diverse yet moving in unity. The movements create waves within the ocean. A Fractal could also represent an enormous marine creature that hosts a vast array of other organisms. All living within the same space within the ocean.

Hear this Truth.

At some point, a particular Fractal chose to express an aspect of itself into human form. This Fractal resides within God. Therefore, Source Creator God, knew of and approved of your unique expression. You were then made manifest through an extraordinary process.

You came here through a Soul.

The Soul

Diagram 5: "A Soul."

The Soul is beyond true comprehension from our third-dimensional perspective. But we can discern its purpose.

Like many things that exist outside of Space Time, the Soul can appear paradoxical and mysterious to us. For example, it is both somewhere and everywhere. It resides within Fractals as a localized cloud of information, and as a vast system of neurons and synapses.

The Soul is a complex structure, and serves many functions that are central to cosmic evolution. It is at once a sentient being, and a technological platform. It acts as a filter, an incarnation mechanism and a birthing-into-matter agent.

There are an infinite number of Souls that generate an infinite number of renditions: human-Avatar or otherwise.

The Soul's central gift and utility is to offer a Fractal a perspective based upon a set of coordinates. It can generate a perspective with mathematical efficiency and precision. Indeed, there is no limit to the choices a Fractal can make when extending an aspect of itself through a Soul.

A simplistic analogy would be that of a Soul representing a massive multigame complex that hosts thousands of video games. And a Fractal, as a gamer, that gets to choose which game to play in, which avatar to assume and which storyline to pursue.

A Soul is also a hub that connects a spectrum of human Avatars together. This is the meaning of the term "Soul family." So, it is not merely a bridge or a portal into form. It is an intelligence center with a support system that allows a Fractal to interface with a vast spectrum of renditions. Some of which will be human-Avatars.

In this Now-life you are connected to a host Soul. Throughout the ages humans have described this special relationship in terms like the Holy Spirit, or angelic guides or a Higher Self. The Frequencies that flow from our Soul to us feel familiar, warm and comforting. There is a great deal of empathy and support available to us that comes from this source.

Ultimately, our Soul is the portal to our Fractal, and to God.

Our Soul is able to mediate between us and our Fractal inter/multidimensionally. It acts as a circuit breaker, compressing the powerful Frequencies that come direct from our Fractal to us. Our Soul plays a key role in our inner spiritual dialogue with our Fractal.

It is what plugs us directly into the Creator.

A Soul functions as a translator between form (Avatars) and non-form (Fractals). It is often our Soul that we first gain contact with when we awaken. It can appear to us as an angelic guide or an ascended teacher, or even a religious figure if that's what an Avatar can relate to best. Although there are many ascended beings in service to humanity that are also available to us. Ours is a rich ecosystem of sentience.

We can think of our relationship to our Soul this way: it's not so much that we have a Soul, it's more that a Soul has us.

It's not always that a "soul family" comes from the same Fractal. For example, we may belong to a human-Avatar group that has the same purpose or set of experiences to learn from but who originate from different Fractals as their source*. This occurs to optimize diversity of choice and experience for a Fractal.

*source as in Fractal, not Source as from God.

For instance, an individual is born into a certain lineage and overtime they are inexplicably drawn to others and move away from their family. This is down to a Soul magnetism, a force that pulls us to others so that we can grow. The ones we are drawn towards carry similar Frequencies to us and share the same mission. This was enabled by incarnation through *the same Soul*.

In this sense then, our Soul offers us a feeling of community, of kinship and of purpose. Just as we have clusters of stars in galaxies, groups of animals that migrate and dwell together, so too we have Soul families.

Within the Soul's complex, multifaceted system, support is offered (guides, intuition, ascended masters) and comfort can be drawn. There is empathy and interest in us personally from our Soul.

We have all experienced it as a warm glimmer of hope on a blue day. It is found in alignment and synchronicity: being in the right place, at the right time, with the right person. It feels warm like home. That's because it is.

Our Higher Power (the most evolved you) resides within our Soul with an eagle's 360 degree view. It is from here that challenges are permitted to come our way, for our greater longterm good. It is here that hard knocks are allowed to occur. It is from here that the doors are opened and blessings, miracles and epiphanies spring from.

Everything comes to us through our Soul to make us stronger, and to bring us into a more profound sense of self-awareness. We are partners as well as participants in the evolutionary process.

Why does a Fractal choose to compress itself and become a human Avatar? We can offer these words: curiosity, meaning, purpose, challenge, perspective, complexity, freedom, and pleasure. In truth, there are as many reasons to incarnate as there are Avatar renditions.

Everything boils down to this: Self-Realization.

From a Fractal's perspective to know everything is to know nothing, to be everywhere is to be nowhere. It is a virgin realm primed for expression, but where does one start? This is the dilemma of omniscience.

Experience offers a Fractal a roadmap. It provides a sense of Self-discovery, of Self-exploration, and even of Self-not-knowing which creates meaning, imparts value and provides purpose.

To understand this better, imagine you had everything you could ever want and were eternal. After a few hundred years of exploring pleasure and manifesting delights, wouldn't you get bored and unmotivated? Wouldn't you crave a puzzle to solve, a challenge to overcome, and others to share your experiences with? Would you not appreciate another's perspective and feedback?

Imagine that experience on a far greater scale.

It's easy to see the extraordinary opportunity that a human Avatar life offers a Fractal. Through an internal generation technology (the Soul) a Fractal can push out through innumerable human Avatars. And as each Avatar is pushed through, it acts like a brain node.

We recommend that you take a break here
and ponder what you have just read.

Avatar: human, node, quest agent, godling

A brain node delivers information and is connected to other brain nodes via junctions called synapses. A human Avatar (node) transmits data through localized experiences and is connected to a network of other Avatars (nodes) through a Frequency network (synapses).

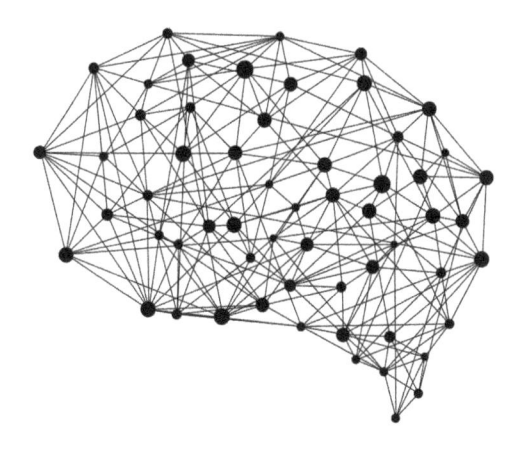

Diagram 6: "Human Node Network."

Clustering information through complex, interconnected parts like this offers a Fractal an opportunity to experience the world of matter within Space and Time, through a certain subjective perspective. There's an enormous freedom of expression and pleasure in this.

Our Fractal knows that nothing it could ever experience through an Avatar would permanently damage it (the Fractal). From the perspective of a "boots on the ground" Avatar however there are real consequences to incarnating with other Avatars.

The unexpected is always present on Earth and that's the thrill of life.

Our Fractal, like nature, can use extremes to activate quantum leaps in Self-Realization. In the natural world this leads to an abundant diversity of life. It may appear that some of these extremes are cruel. For example, some species will become extinct after a catastrophe but in reality they are never truly lost.

Right now, dinosaurs are roaming the Earth. The Dodo blissfully pecks at bugs in the grass. They exist within their Now-moments. Everything is everywhere, all at once. It's just that from our Avatar Now-perspective we cannot see them.

Extremes of adversity can be useful to drive quantum leaps in consciousness. In an individual and in an entire species. But suffering need not be a long term strategy. It has a role like a tool in the tool box. Rudimentary and useful but not the only one we can select.

Suffering is like the saw, and adversity the hammer that knocks a block of wood into shape. Then comes the chisel, gentle in the master's touch. Then comes the oil cloth. Then comes the platform. Then comes the glory of a public exhibition. Then the artisan starts again on something new. This is the goal of our Fractal: increased Self-Realization, a spectrum of experiences at a time.

Our Fractal will choose our adversaries as thoughtfully as it chooses our beloveds. Indeed, our foes often serve us more faithfully. Adversaries represent the finer tools of impression.

Of course, this doesn't excuse poor behavior in others. Nor does it mean we should surrender to abuse.

But human Avatars are not helpless pawns on a chess board.

Consciousness is the name of the game, and as an Avatar awakens it gains more autonomy. In terms of adversaries, the key is to identify the teacher quickly. To see that what he or she projects is something that exists inside of us. Something that was formerly hidden. Conflict dissolves under epiphany. The "aha" moment releases the charge and the teacher from their role.

Wisdom is the ability to know the lesson before it needs to traumatize us. It's seeing an assassin on a distant hill acknowledging them then moving swiftly in another direction. Wisdom begets enlightenment. Enlightenment needn't feel woo-woo. Enlightenment simply opens up more choices. It's a wider bandwidth.

Forgiveness of oneself and all others is the quickest path to enlightenment. It is no small thing. When we forgive someone, we set them free. We release them from the bondage of indebtedness to us, and in doing so we release ourselves.

Why should we forgive others? We should contemplate forgiveness because we have wounded others as much as we have been wounded. Often we have wounded others in ignorance (unconsciousness). Forgiveness is like the amnesty declared at the end of a world war. The bugle sounds and every soldier on every battlefield lays down his weapon and goes home.

Osmosis is the return home.

At death, our Soul will attempt to bring us back home to our Fractal. This is restorative for the Avatar. It is the meaning of heaven. For the Fractal it is informative. The experiences of the Avatar are synthesized into itself. This is Self-Realization.

But many Avatars loop back onto the Earth through unconscious recycling. Fractals allow this out of respect for their free will and an adherence to the Law of Cause and Effect. This is the wheel of Samsara spoken about in Buddhism. Karma is simply an accounting system attached to Cause and Effect. A tally of the consequences of our actions.

So, violent, traumatic and narcissistic behaviors produce and are the consequence of low-Frequencies. They pull us further away from our Soul and Fractal.

They also create effects. If an Avatar persists in perpetrating negative actions towards others, they will fall into deeper unconsciousness and will automatically default into recycled unconscious incarnations, until they can return to consciousness.

Some Avatars have a special role to play. This is to awaken, to self-realize, to act as a catalyst in a family or a social group. They can also possess a redemptive quality: to find and call back into consciousness those formerly lost to unconsciousness.

This is redemption. It is salvation which literally means "to come home."

When we awaken we can act as a catalyst for others. We can help members of our Soul family to return home. Return to our Fractal is through our Soul. It acts as the mediator and gateway. This is what the word Synthesis represents: to bring all aspects (Avatars) back into the whole.

Avatars act as Time Stamps of experience. They play an important geographical role in a Fractal's consciousness, offering it a map of individuation. This is highly desirable, delectable even because a Fractal is the totality of all of its single units - like the value of a single ant to its colony.

What is the value of a single ant to its colony? An ant can map out a vast terrain by crawling all over it. Each crawl creates a map that the hive mind can self-assemble and use to comprehend the totality of its domain.

As Avatars we are more than a crawling ant. We have access to wider fields of consciousness while in human form. We call these the Three Spheres.

Contemplation and Journal section

What Teachings Resonated With Me in This Section?
Why?
How Does This Affect Me?

The Three Spheres

This chapter at a glance:

- The Three Spheres: Awake Time; the Dreamscape; the In-between Spaces before Birth, and after Death.

The Three Spheres

The human form was created to experience matter as bound by gravity in a dense, emotion and sensory rich environment. Our five senses are the portals through which we interact with this environment. Earth is a Free Will Zone and you came here understanding that:

- All actions are permissible.
- All actions have consequences.
- We are subject to the consequences of our actions.
- Others are subject to our actions.
- We are subject to the actions of others.
- We are subject to random experiences beyond our control.

Without these coordinates within a Free Will Zone new experiences could not be generated. By being born as a human on Earth, we accept these terms. This fact relieves us from questions like:

- Why do bad things happen?
- Why does God allow bad things to happen?
- Why have bad things happened to me?

Simply put, bad things happening was the risk you were prepared to take in exchange for rapid, evolutionary growth in a Free Will Zone.

This doesn't excuse the bad choices some humans make that cause suffering. It doesn't mean we should tolerate poor behavior. It doesn't mean that negative actions can be done without consequences. All choices, positive or negative come with repercussions.

A Free Will Zone is perfect for the spontaneous, rapid and diverse flow of life. You not only chose this theater of experience. You are one of its architects.

Humans experience life through three Spheres. These are:

1. Awake Time.
2. The Dreamscape.
3. The In-between Spaces before Birth, and after Death.

Awake Time

The first Sphere of influence is Awake Time, which is the time when you are not asleep. This may feel self-evident although to many it is not, because we are often unawake during Awake Time. The average person's Awake Time is around 95% unconscious.

So, in any given moment when you are not asleep you are in fact unconscious. It's a form of sleepwalking. How is this experienced?

Think about an average week/work day. What time do you get up? What do you do upon waking? Go over your actions. Most of what we do is a series of motions that are performed without thought. We default into the same programs of behavior, of habits, and thought-forms.

Same thing, different day.

Over time, a human life lived mostly unconsciously can resemble a series of interlocking loops: the week, the weekend, vacation, daytime, eveningtime, night time, childhood, adulthood, old age. Decades of repeating the familiar produces a zombified existence that can feel painfully vacuous in the brief moments of clarity or consciousness humans experience.

It is easy to see why people drift off into fantasies and are not present with others. At the root of the problem is that unconsciousness untethers us from the Earth's electromagnetic field. Unconscious, habitual behavior separates us from our body, which in turn, dislocates us from our place in Space Time. This is experienced in a sense of "not being here," or feeling adrift.

Our modern world is set up to push us into full-blown unconsciousness. It is engineered to pull us out of our bodies. Otherwise its agents and merchants would have no control over us. This is the reason so many people feel empty.

It is why they seek fulfillment outside of themselves. Why they take substances to enhance their experiences. Why they stay busy-busy-busy. Why they seek a deeper connection to their bodies through others. Only the more they do this, the greater the inner void becomes.

This is because materialism is unsustainable and leads to despair. Attachments and an obsession for security leaves us vanquished and miserable. Humans were not designed to live like this.

Awake Time was meant to be a magical interaction with the physical world. It was an opportunity to vividly experience emotions, engage with others and execute ideas into form. It's a creation space, where we get to do things. Every day was meant to be lived afresh with unique opportunities and challenges.

The Simplicity Platform 8 Tenets is designed for our Awake Time. It is a technology for daily life. It guides us back into our bodies and the present-moment. Our Point of Now is where consciousness exists.

Embodiment is the key. Our human bodies are immovable. They reside within Space Time, always perfectly located. Our bodies do not leave us. We leave them and in doing so, we untether from the Earth, which holds our Frequency location throughout the cosmos.

The Simplicity Platform 8 Tenets is the foundation of Kaya Usher's Frequency Technology. The Waves take us deeper into our Awake Time by rooting us even more firmly into the present-moment. It is exacting and potent. It does this by stirring things up that we'd rather not face or were unaware of. It will ask us to shine a light into the darkest places of our mind. Why and How does The Waves do this?

Why The Waves does this?

Consciousness is all-seeing, all-knowing, irrespective of what is being viewed. It cannot exist in delusion or denial. That's the domain of the unconscious. The term *ignorance is bliss* has some truth to it. Truth can be unpleasant, especially if it involves us taking action, or taking a risk.

Truth reconnects us to aspects of ourselves that dwell in unconsciousness. It is the equivalent of a lighthouse on a moonless night. We are often too busy to stop and go over challenging times. In fact, most of us would prefer to avoid unpleasant memories altogether.

But if we are to return home upon death *as light as a feather* (whole) it is extremely important that we have pulled back in every aspect of ourselves (unconscious) that were left behind in Time Stamps. Particularly aspects like a wounded child.

How The Waves does this

The Waves pull things into your electromagnetic field that you cannot ignore. If you are not ready for big changes you should return to the 8 Tenets as a practice. The changes the 8 Tenets support are gentler, occurring over a longer period of time.

On the other hand, if you are ready to pull in every unconscious aspect of yourself into your electromagnetic field, The Waves will facilitate and accelerate that for you. Memories and feelings will surface that require processing.

Circumstances will arise that will demand a decision, a direction. The effect of people, places and things upon you in the past will become self-evident. Situations that you once put up with will become intolerable.

Simultaneously, things that you didn't think were possible will enter your field, challenging you to take risks and push harder. People that resonate where you're headed will appear in your life. A new location or a change of career may suddenly draw you inexplicably.

What we are talking about here are catalytic, paradigm shifts. It requires the kind of "work" that most people choose to take over many lifetimes. Through The Waves you will be given an opportunity to make a quantum leap in one lifetime. It's efficient.

This is a technology that is also designed to enter the Dreamscape. Our second Sphere of influence.

The Dreamscape

Compared to Awake Time, the Dreamscape is like a cave that's been hidden from us for thousands of years. Yet, it occupies a third of our day, a third of our life. Just stop and think about how much time you spend sleeping? Why does this Sphere exist? What is its purpose?

The Dreamscape was created for three reasons.

1. To reset the human body each day.
2. To process unresolved desires, fears, situations from our day.
3. To journey untethered into other realities as a preparation for death.

The first two reasons for the Dreamscape are self-evident, but the third may not be as obvious. During deep sleep we are able to travel beyond our five-sensory world. This isn't an Out of Body Experience (OBE); it's an Inner Body Experience (IBE) because the human body is a portal into other dimensions.

Through this portal we experience an enormous range of realities without actually dying. Some realities resemble

Awake Time, some are more elevated spaces and some are denser, even Hellish places.

Some of our unconscious aspects, especially the ones from a traumatizing childhood, can reside in what appear to be Hellish places. Aspects of ourselves lost during intoxication or severe accidents can also be dislodged in dark, unconscious spaces and these may show themselves to us in scary dreams. In such dreams we may find ourselves distorted or acting out of character. However, what we are encountering is an unconscious part of ourselves. One that longs to be seen and heard and synthesized.

Keeping a dream diary is helpful in identifying the age of the unconscious aspect and the surroundings they reveal themselves in. With the discipline of a detective, we can recover all of the unconscious aspects of ourselves in this lifetime, through dream recall. Some find lucid dreaming particularly useful in this respect.

Bringing our awareness into the Dreamscape more fully will enable us to navigate these realms while staying grounded in who we are, tethered to our bodies and connected to the Earth. There is no greater preparation for death than this.

There are many misconceptions around death. Death is not a place. It is an action. It is a technique that can be understood and experienced without fear, like birth. There is no rehearsal. It is a one-time act.

But we can prepare for it. As of writing, there is a book, *The Art of Dying* which we intend to create and share in the future.

For now, we would say that The Waves will pull you more deeply into your dreams and pull your dreams more deeply into you. It will flush up the unconscious aspects that generate nightmares, and bring them home.

This is a Synthesis through Osmosis.

It is the work most Avatars do after death. This is what the Life Review represents. But this elongates the evolutionary process.

We can do this work now. Every 24-hours you dip your toes into these preparatory spaces when you sleep. So pay close attention to what The Waves shows you through your dreams. Notice any shifts in your dreams, themes, locations, lucidity. Journal what you experience in your Dreamscape. No matter what you experience, just observe and process at your own pace.

The purpose is not to attain full lucidity within the Dreamscape, although for some this may be beneficial. It's to bring in more connectivity between your awake time and asleep time. Your Dreamscape is not another's. It is a reflection and extension of the greater You. A space to go deeper into. It is the land of redemption. Where lost unconscious aspects of ourselves are found.

Your dreams are also vehicles through which you can release the darker, more dysfunctional aspects of yourself. Dreams are incredible opportunities to hold these aspects longer in the light of Awake Time. Where full consciousness exists undisturbed. We never judge a dream. It's a window to look through.

The third Sphere of experience and influence is vast and mostly unknowable to humans. These represent the In-between Spaces before Birth, and after Death. Where you dwell when not a human being.

It is not someplace out there, it exists within. The human body is a vehicle of high multidimensional value, and the female body is a divine portal through which all humans must enter. It is the holiest of vessels. The Zero Point to and from the In-between Spaces.

The In-between Spaces are other realities, planes of existence that our Fractal creates to experience all manner of things. Some of these realms are populated by non-human entities, non-physical entities and multidimensional beings. At your deepest level you feel this Space. It is your true home.

Take a break here, breathe, relax and clear your mind.

Contemplation and Journal section

What Teachings Resonated With Me in This Section?
Why?
How Does This Affect Me?

The Principles: Avatar Mechanics

This chapter at a glance:

- Spiritual: Resonance, Teachers, Practices.
- Physical: Breath, Hydration, Nutrition, Movement.
- Emotional: Experienced and Expressed, Relationships.
- Sexual: Divine Partnerships, Pleasure, Reproduction.
- Mental: Intellectual, Creative, Analytical.

The Principles: Avatar Mechanics

There is no other technology in existence that surpasses the potential for expression, experience and evolution than the human body. Modern humans are not taught how to utilize this technology, although breakthroughs in epigenetics and neuroscience are shifting this.

Knowing what our potential is, is particularly pertinent in an age of AI obsession. Our body surpasses anything that AI could ever claim to deliver.

The human body is configured into five main systems. The Principles are a set of guides to these systems and are explored in greater detail in another offering. In The Waves book we present an overview.

The five main systems are:

1. Spiritual: resonance, teachers, practices.
2. Physical: breath, hydration, nutrition, movement.
3. Emotional: experienced and expressed, relationships.
4. Sexual: divine partnerships, pleasure, reproduction.
5. Mental: intellectual, creative, analytical.

1

Spiritual: resonance, teachers, practices

Everything that enters our electromagnetic field affects our body because everything resonates. The resonance of everything impacts the resonance of everything. Resonance is vibrational and magnetic, like our bodies. It manifests within the human body as sensations, feelings and emotions.

For example, food carries a resonance. After a meal have you ever felt exhausted or depleted? That's because the food we consumed carried a lower resonance to our own. Processing a lower-Frequency food takes energy from our body. We can keep a food diary and even learn to feel the difference in the resonance of foods before we eat them.

Media is another resonance influencer. What you watch, consume and engage with will alter your electromagnetic field. What kinds of content are you attracted to? It's worth contemplating because your media tastes indicate a Frequency match with your own resonance level.

Our bodies are around 60% water. Doctor Masaru Emoto's experiments with water propose that water is able to *respond* to human emotion, thoughts, words and written messages. But water also carries its own Frequencies that are dependent on where it was sourced, what treatments it went through and how it was stored and delivered. Our water's resonance is essential to our well-being. Carefully consider what water you take into your body.

The most potent resonance influence comes from other humans.

For instance, most of us will know within seconds of meeting someone if they are a resonance match or not. Some describe this as a gut feeling or intuition. That's true because those systems exist within your body's electromagnetic field and are triggered by another's. If you feel overpowered, tired or even depressed around an individual that's because their resonance is creating friction in your field.

Teachers often possess powerful, enlarged electromagnetic fields. It's what draws people to them. A teacher's field can impact us negatively or positively.

If a teacher's electromagnetic field is negative it will draw energy from us. It will give us something in return but with a hook, leaving us energetically hungry because the "fix" is temporary. In such a case, we will feel addicted to the teacher, even obsessed with them. We may not notice this at first.

As with all parasitic relationships there's a love-bombing that happens in the beginning. This is where a teacher and the control source behind the teacher bombards a person's electromagnetic field with higher resonating, bliss-inducing Frequencies. It's a temporary high.

Gradually though we will begin to feel stifled and controlled. We may feel exhausted and empty, after time spent with our teacher. We may feel pressured to part with our money or gifts in the service of a teacher. In most cases we can guarantee you that your body knew the teacher was negative and tried to warn you many times.

Our bodies can always detect the purity of another's electromagnetic field. We will get mixed messages. We will feel uncomfortable with some of the practices. A teacher who holds a high-resonating electromagnetic field needs nothing from you.

Your body will feel calm and grounded in that person's presence. And when the time comes for you to graduate from the relationship, your teacher will bless you. Our body has an innate wisdom and The Waves asks us to trust that.

2

Physical: breath, hydration, nutrition, movement

Our body needs oxygen through fresh air. Practice breathing deeply, expanding your diaphragm and filling your belly. Small children know how to breathe. They walk with their bellies out like a Buddha, because they are connected to Life Force.

Spend time outside in the sunlight and in all weathers because it nourishes our lungs and skin which are one connected organ. Breath should flow naturally, not forced or controlled. There are many modalities that teach how to breathe. You should always feel a resonance match to what you're learning. No two breaths are alike, like waves breaking on the beach. So we allow each breath to flow in and out to our own rhythm.

We are electromagnetic beings and water is essential to our structure. Clean, naturally structured water is the best way to replenish. If we cannot access artisan water we can purchase good filters. We can explore traditional ways to cleanse our water of heavy metals, chemicals and contaminants. We can let our water sit in the sun. Sunlight purifies water. We can bless our water and shift its Frequency resonance. This is restructuring through words.

Our body needs high-resonance nourishment in order to maintain its vitality. We do not recommend a particular diet to follow that is optimum because everyone's body is different. For some, a diet rich in animal protein and fruit is best. For others, a plant-based diet works more efficiently. There are many to choose from. What's important is where our food comes from.

We can ask:

- Was this food created with the highest intentions?
- How does it leave me feeling?

All foods carry a Frequency. You can develop your sensory skills by pausing before you choose a food for consumption and feeling it. Kaya Usher calls this "tapping in" which is a resonance taste test. Hold the food item. Look at it. Is it vibrant? In time, we can even develop an ability to see a food item's inner glow. Everything generates an electromagnetic field. Everything impacts you.

Our body needs to move and not just in exercise or sports. It needs to sway, to stretch, to swing, and to dance. Movement keeps everything in flow. Find regular moments in your day to move. Follow your heart's desires. If you want to bop or skip, do so. Motion is the pulse of our Life Force, so move - move - move.

3

Emotional: experienced and expressed, relationships

All emotions are valid. They are like the weather. There's a place for rain and sunshine. Storms bring forth rainbows. Frost kills decaying vegetation. Forest fires replenish the soil.

Similarly, every emotion has its function. They were intended to blow in and blow out. When we allow our emotions to express and the caveat here is *express appropriately* the charge gets released with minimal collateral damage.

An emotion was not intended to linger or get stuck in our body. It wasn't designed to resonate and lead to a blockage, a disease or a permanent state. If not cleared, sour moods can solidify into a suffocating depression that rolls on and on.

Many of us are not responsible for the original emotional resonances that get stuck in our electromagnetic field. Commonly they were created in our childhoods and accompanied by trauma and suffering. These leave a residue in the form of a resonance, like a Frequency scar. Trauma release work and therapeutic practices can do much to support shifting historic blockages.

Kaya Usher has helped countless individuals to Clean Up Their Space (electromagnetic field) using her Frequency Technology: the 8 Tenets. From a Frequency perspective, it is possible to edit our holographic form within this third-dimensional rendition.

Many have experienced a dynamic shift and discovered a profound relief that is permanent. We strongly recommend that anyone experiencing the effects of childhood trauma or severe depression and anxiety to seek medical and therapeutic support in conjunction with Kaya Usher's Frequency Technology work.

> "We can use nature to ground any lingering emotions of sadness, of emptiness, of blankness, of loss. Nature is a great regulator. Its frequency will harmonize ours. It is self-sustaining, eternal, and aware. I can go into nature if I feel overwhelmed."
> Kaya Usher Free To Be 365.

Balance is the key. We were not designed to be emotional tornedos swirling from one extreme to another. Neither were we meant to be androids. Humans were created to be fluid on all things.

4

Sexual: divine partnerships, pleasure, reproduction

Sexual embodiment is a powerful key for evolution. It was created for our joy and pleasure, but first and foremost, the human body is a holy vessel. A powerful vehicle of electromagnetic energy. We do well to bear this in mind when we are intimate with another, equally powerful vehicle.

When we are sexually intimate we are not just opening up our physical body. We are allowing access to specific energy centers. Our partner's energy centers temporarily become one with ours. Certain Frequencies entangle, and waves flow together.

Our body issues red flags around sexuality. For example, if one of a sexual partnership is left exhausted after sex this is because there has been an energy harvest through a partner's energy centers. Sex may be used as a way to control a partner. The occasion for sex may be an unconscious desire like lust which is a lower-Frequency, or it can feel sacrificial. A partner may even feel abused during intercourse. This implies that their partner's conscious or unconscious intent was negative.

It's important to listen to our body. If something doesn't feel good we should stop. If there is the potential for co-creation (conception) with a sexual partner, we should ask if it's for our highest good, or the good of a child?

In the modern world sex is offered as a commodity. We have also been taught that sexuality has a specific location. A few organs here, some erogenous zones there. Where the same steps lead to an end destination and a chemical charge is released. And that sex has a dual function of pleasure and procreation, but this perspective limits us.

Sex is meant to be sacred. It has the potential to open interdimensional portals throughout the body, and to collapse Space Time for a few seconds. The key component is our heart. If we connect with another through our heart *first* we can open our entire electromagnetic field to them. That is a significant gift because an open electromagnetic field electrifies the entire body.

This type of sexual connection becomes holistic without any loss of energy from either partner. It is a continuum of pleasure that builds and flows. Its crescendo is a Free Fall. An implosion into a co-created Zero Point. This is the total surrender of one person to another, vice versa. Sexual connection, when engaged with high-integrity, reinvigorates and expands the electromagnetic field, and it does not follow a programmed formula.

5

Mental: intellectual, creative, analytical

Many of us begin our Frequency journey by clearing the headspace. It is an important step because distortions run riot there. Our minds are powerful projectors and manifestors. They can loop programs and project them out into reality.

But our headspace was created to be a processing center. It was designed to be efficient, proficient, sharp, concise and balanced. That means that information flows in and information flows out. We don't allow things to settle, then stick and loop. This means living without attachment to outcomes. We Free Fall in every moment so that nothing attaches itself to us.

When we live without attachments, that is, without interference, we experience mental coherence which is Harmonic Resonance. This feels like a deep, vibrational calm.

Our brain is one entity. It is not divided into two sections: Left Brain, Right Brain. This is an artificial separation. The greatest thinkers and visionaries used all of their brain.

Cerebral unity unleashes an enormous amount of energy to our intellects, and imbibes critical thinking with creative imagination.

How can we unify our brain?

We can practice being ambidextrous and lean in on our weak areas. If we are creative and math or science isn't our thing we can begin studying those subjects in ways that are fun and adventurous. If we are predominantly mathematical and logical we can take up a musical instrument or a creative hobby. It's not a case of "going back to school" but of "learning never ends." We stay curious, and playful like children. There is always something else to learn.

Our body is a marvel.

The five primary systems that govern our human experience work together as one technology. If we learn to trust our body, and stay faithful to it - that is, fully embodied - we will take charge of our evolution.

There's a memoir called *The Camel Knows the Way*, which chronicles an incredible journey back to God. We would say, *Your Body Knows the Way* every single time. So let go and trust.

Contemplation and Journal section

What Teachings Resonated With Me in This Section? Why?
How Does This Affect Me?

Activation: Grounding Golden Sovereign Technique

We close out each Section with this activation. Grounding connects us more deeply to the Earth's electromagnetic field. This enables us to hold and sustain an expanded bandwidth of consciousness.

Get comfortable.
Hold or look at your natural inanimate object/s.
They are our Frequency partners.
Present to remind us of our own deep resonance.
Solid, perfect, and pure.
Feel the Frequencies they run.
They are tethered to our Earth.
Just as we are always tethered to our Earth.
In permanence.

Grounding Golden Sovereign Technique

Grounding ...
We are grounded to the Earth.

Golden
We are filled with Golden Filaments.

Sovereign
Our system belongs to us and us alone.

Technique
Our technique to use always.

Count down from 33 to zero and visualize your own Frequency network.

- Your Golden Filaments.
- Your Holy Waters.
- Your Sphere.
- Your Waves.

Count down out loud.
33 32 31 30 29 28 27 26 25 24 23 22 21
20 19 18 17 16 15 14 13 12 11
10 9 8 7 6 5 4 3 2 1 Zero

Your inanimate objects.
Hold them in each hand.

Ask aloud:
Can I be as solid as this stone?
As light as this feather?
Show me how.

Say aloud:
Teach me through stillness.
Guide me through humility.
Show me through service.

Ask aloud:
How can I tether more deeply to this Earth?

Now go there.
Feel that.
Be there always.

Safe - connected - activated - grounded.

INTEGRATION

We recommend that you take at least
one week away from this book.

Reflections on Osmosis

Ponder on the following or create some concepts from Section 2 in the following notes section.

"What is this I AM?

It is You as a Fractal with its own God-given Blueprint, aglow and shimmering. Just like a fingerprint, it is unique and one of a kind.

Then, it is you as part of a Soul.
It is you as an awake Avatar."
What comes up for you when you think about your I AM?

"Free Fall does not require that you give anything of yourself away in order to reach enlightenment. So separate letting go of all attachments to sacrifice."
What does Free Fall mean to you?

"It is possible to recircuit, to release the charge behind a trauma and release it from our electromagnetic field. Once it's released, the trigger is removed and we are liberated from that moment in Space Time."
How does this statement make you feel?

Practice Ideas:

- Record yourself reading the poem titled "If" and listen as often as you are called. Notice what areas make you uncomfortable or cause anxiety and then lean into those areas until there is no friction around them.
- Use your breath to bring you more deeply into your body and the present moment. Feeling your chest rise and fall. Letting go of any resistance.
- Notice if you are given any insights into your dreamscape. Journal anything that you remember or what comes up for you.
- Continue to practice grounding techniques and connecting with your natural objects. The Earth is here to help us and is our partner in this process.

Remember that Osmosis is the process of bringing traumas and lost parts of ourselves home. It takes patience, it takes non-judgement, it takes forgiveness.

Remember that you are loved.

Contemplation and Journal section

Osmosis Notes:

Section 3

Transfiguration

"A state of embodiment where we bring in all of the elements through Imprints into our Blueprint through Synthesis." Kaya Usher The Waves course

Section 3: Transfiguration

Contents:

- Harmonic Resonance.
- The Golden Filaments.
- The Waves, You and Everything Else.
- You and God.
- Grounding Golden Sovereign Technique.
- A Prayer.

Activation: Harmonic Resonance

Harmonic Resonance is a technique that gets us in the pocket. In Section 3 we will take the training wheels off. It is time to embody Harmonic Resonance. This is an internal act of coherence. We cannot do that for you. But together we can join one another and resonate in communion.

Let's get in position.
Settle down.
Get comfortable.
We will count down from 21 to zero.
Counting entrains our monkey mind into stillness and at the same time we follow the natural flow of our breath.

Feel your body, that's your Avatar.
A holy vessel.
(Count down)
21 20 19 18 17 16 15 14 13 12
11 10 9 8 7 6 5 4 3 2 1 - Zero

These words will activate your

- Electromagnetic field
- Golden Filaments
- Holy Waters
- Spheres

Free Fall through silence into Zero Point.
In silence count down from 21 to zero.
21 20 19 18 17 16 15 14 13 12 11
10 9 8 7 6 5 4 3 2 1 - Zero
(Pause for a few seconds here)

Spheres.
Velocity.
Magnetism.
Spin.
Circle.
Light.

Harmonic Resonance is a vibration.
We can allow it to resonate within our body.
Hum "AUM" 21 times.
This will amplify your Frequencies.

(Fall into silence for as long as called to)

The Golden Filaments

This chapter at a glance:

- The Sentient Connectivity of All Things.
- Earth is a Multiplayer Free Will Zone.
- The Many Roles We Play.
- Open Systems and Closed Systems.
- Forgiveness is the Key to Escaping a Closed System.

The Golden Filaments

Welcome to this part of the book. We have entered Section 3: Transfiguration.

Transfiguration means a change in form or appearance. It comes as a consequence of Embodiment. In Section 2: Osmosis we learned that when we embody we give physical form (Avatar) to that which is non-physical (Soul, Fractal) because our Fractal is the Cause and human Form is its Effect. The mediator of these states is our Soul.

This is a Divine Structure of Order.

Transfiguration is a return to the One, having quested to become Everything. This is a replication of the Divine Structure of Order.

Out of the One came All. Therefore separation is a holy act, a Free Fall into Loss. Our innate desire for sovereignty and independence from a control source is God-given. It is not a sin.

In the beginning of Space Time, Creator released aspects of itself in spirals that sprouted in every direction like solar flares pushing Fractals of itself out into nurseries. Clusters of Fractals nested together in pods along the spirals.

Creator released these Fractals without attachment, without intention in Free Will. Fractals are autonomous. Creator did this not knowing what lay ahead in order to know IT-Self more deeply out of unconditional Love.

The first Frequency is Love. Love begets Love. Fractals were birthed in Love and held within the Golden Filaments.

The Golden Filaments hold everything together like a fine silk tapestry. They are sentient synapses that fill the Holy Waters of God. The Golden Filaments form a conscious network and collectively represent the Mind of the Creator. These Filaments transmit information from being to being, from Fractal cluster to Fractal cluster, moving in all directions.

Everything is connected.
As Above so Below.

Fractals choose to orbit and journey in clusters. Avatars choose to home together in Souls like shoals of fish. Everything is social. We are bound by mutually aligned Frequency fields in order to circle and intersect in innumerable, interesting ways within realities that we have collectively created.

The Golden Filaments connect all things within a substance that is the Holy Waters of God. Pulses create Frequencies, Frequencies form waves, waves manifest form and all within a Divine Ocean.

We swim in the same Holy Waters as everything, and everyone else. So everything that applies to you in The Waves applies to every other person that crosses your path. It applies to every single human on this planet. It applies to every individual that has ever lived and ever will live. Our waves interact with other waves.

We chose to manifest form with others because this is what generates a diversity of experiences. It is also an evolutionary technique. Every other person is a reflection of us. Holding an aspect that we cannot see within our Fractal because it is too immense. They show us our blindspots. Places from which we can grow.

Some Avatars are bound to us magnetically through a bloodline. In fact, many of our friends, if we traced our lineages back, share a common ancestor with us. There is a magnetic draw that pulls people together.

More powerful are the Frequency fields that draw Avatars together. These are the friends that we recognize as our soul tribe. These people feel immediately like "home." This is because we share the same Soul and Fractal. Generally, we are less entangled to these soul tribe people and freer to grow together in equality.

Many Fractals choose to incarnate groups of Avatars together to push evolutionary growth through extremes. These roles are chosen before birth, which at a Fractal level is a set of archetypes and a set of engagements that are mapped out and then generated within a shared lifetime.

These groups can go this way or that as each Avatar is endowed with a free will. This gives life on Earth an element of unpredictability, spontaneity and surprise. Think about the many archetypes you have played over countless lifetimes?

The hero, the villain, the lover, and the martyr to name but a few. These roles offered our Fractal experiences but they also required partners: counterparts, allies and adversaries. In the past those experiences may have been binary and short-lived. Someone wins if someone loses.

The Waves offers us the opportunity to escape these binary, repetitive options. When we become more fully embodied and expand our consciousness we hold more sovereignty. That means we wield more velocity, more electromagnetism. This opens up a wider bandwidth with more options to us. We are no longer locked into an unconscious game of life.

Life on Earth is a holographic game simulation and the more we enhance through consciousness the more we attract conscious Avatars like ourselves. This is "raising our game" because our group has raised its Frequencies. This is very important to understand because certain mechanics are at play.

Multiplayer lives come with consequences. The Waves frees us from superstitions and external control sources. It puts the power back in our hands but it also holds us accountable. For once we have seen we cannot unsee the role we have played so many times in our own experiences and in the experiences of others.

We literally wake up from a long, deep sleep of multiple incarnations.

This is consciousness.

Earth represents a holographic game simulation. What do we mean by this? We mean that as co-creators, we as Fractals created experiential spaces. They resemble the world shown in the movie *The Matrix*. These experiential spaces host two primary systems: a Closed System and an Open System. Both systems can resonate in the same space. Earth is one such space.

Unconscious humans are locked into a Closed System. We have all at one time or another experienced a Closed System. It's the sensation of GroundHog Day, a carousel ride. Where we live but evolve little, then die and forget who we are. After death we get recycled back with the same players and we reenact the same dramas.

In a Closed System lifetime after lifetime is spent as variations on a theme. The roles may be reversed but the experiences' scope of growth is capped. In fact, Closed Systems can only offer us diminishing returns of awareness and those lives can become entire epochs of looping. It is represented as a closed circle or the ouroboros.

Fractals prefer to incarnate Avatars that are fluid, that can move and pivot and interact with other Avatars dynamically. This is an Open System and its trajectory is represented as a multi-faceted spiral, where an Avatar can move in any direction at will. We can visualize this as Golden Ratio, interconnected Fibonacci spirals.

Opportunities are rich in Open Systems. Avatars that operate here attract one another and collaborate to take on loftier ambitions. Ambitions that can involve a great many people, and when done optimally create huge waves of change. Shifting the destiny of an entire nation, even an entire solar system.

If our life feels like a loop we can choose at any moment to move from a Closed System to an Open System. There are three ways, each one equally as important:

1. We dedicate ourselves to becoming more conscious in every area of our lives.
2. We take responsibility for our role in previous and contemporary experiences.
3. We forgive ourselves and every person we have ever magnetized into our experiences.

Some of us have accumulated debts because of the way we have lived our lives. A debt is an action or behavior we have perpetrated that has harmed another. This is what is referred to as karma. Forgiveness from the wounded party releases us from this debt.

Before we awaken and become conscious, our debts against others are automatically repaid by unconscious reincarnation. In other words, if nothing is learned from a lifetime we unconsciously incarnate back into a similar life plan along with the people we are indebted to. It is easy to see how this system could soon become redundant. The Frequency equivalent of Tic Tac Toe.

Unconditional forgiveness releases everyone involved from a Closed Circuit. So, if one player wakes up, the unconscious game is over. The loop that binds everyone will be broken. What happens to the people in our lives that remain unconscious? This needn't concern us. The unconscious will seek out the unconscious until an awakening situation is triggered.

All experiences are a call to consciousness. The same is as true in a general dynamic as it is in a family dynamic. Meaning, that we can release ourselves from a bullying authority figure, let's say a mean person that keeps showing up as a boss in our career in the same way that we can release ourselves from a bullying parent.

First, we step back and see *our role* in the dynamic. Why are we drawing a domineering co-partner into our life? What are we meant *to change about ourselves* in order to release that individual from our journey?

We turn attention away from the perpetrator, the things they're doing, and we concentrate entirely within. All change must come from inside of us before it can resonate outwards to shift our reality. We needn't concern ourselves with the details. The details (externals) will organize themselves.

Consciousness is the game-changer.

We can break out of any Closed System by going within. We can resonate away from any negative situation. When we stay resonating at the same level as the person or issue we are signaling our consent.

So resonate away from anyone that you no longer need to learn from. When we release ourselves from a Closed System we liberate our loved ones. Everyone who came before. Everyone here with you. Everyone who will come after is set free. It's like a massive web of chains gets torn apart.

The great teachers understood this when they preached forgiveness.

They were sending out a truth wave that reverberated through the beatitudes into the hearts of their followers. They were embodying a Frequency that could free their listeners just by being in their presence. They literally vibrated an electromagnetic field that entrained their followers to free themselves from the tangled reeds of karma.

In no small way, we can do the same. Through forgiveness we can send out truth waves that will impact our loved ones and even release people that we regard as enemies, as oppressors from having to repeat the same loop over and over again.

This latter action is one of undeserved kindness. It is a gift of Grace. This type of awareness embodies a higher Law, a greater Truth. It holds as much significance as the moving of planets. It is a God-inspired action that involves letting go of an enormous magnitude. Yet, that is where true freedom resides.

It's in the forgiveness where all sins are washed away.

The Hebrew word for sin means at its root, a missing of the mark, as in being off target. It is an archery term. So, when we forgive we release a burden from those who simply missed their target for awakening. And in the same moment a great weight is removed from us. As we shift everything shifts around us. That is what we are talking about here: waves upon waves upon waves.

Some transgressions may feel too burdensome to forgive. Their gravitas is such that we may not even feel it's possible. This can be true of a serious trauma to ourselves or of a loved one at the hands of another. But we are not asked to walk this path alone. We can request help from our Soul, from our Fractal which is our Higher Self, and from God - the Source of All. Whatever feels more comfortable to us.

We can simply be open to the idea of forgiveness.

There is much compassion for us little Avatars, the boots on the ground crew down here. We can surrender what is beyond us to something greater. Here is a master key to forgiveness. When we Free Fall into ourselves. When we let go of all resistance. We automatically fall into a state of Grace.

For the individual who has perpetrated the harm or wrongs against yourself and others there will be a personal reckoning, which is an opportunity to awaken. But that has nothing to do with us.

If we have wounded or significantly wronged another, we will come to understand that there are consequences to our actions, even unconscious ones. This is the Law of Cause and Effect. If we surrender to the wisdom of the consequences, we won't be entangled by this process.

Ultimately, Transfiguration is the consequence of a process. One that gains momentum and traction over time. Leaps often arise from a small act of faith or kindness. Tipping us into an elevated state of being.

Self-forgiveness is an integral part. The Waves come without judgment. It asks only that we be honest with ourselves. That we are willing to open the lid on things that we've avoided for years. It offers us a chance to release the energy from all of the people, places and things before we cross over in death.

So that we might, as the ancient Egyptians advised, *be as light as a feather.* And we would add, be *as solid as a rock.* That's the formula for a superlative, harmoniously aligned-death.

Kaya Usher's Frequency Technology will get you in position in-the-here-and-now and in every other place where you exist. It will bring you tighter into embodiment so that you become more efficient in an Open System of Avatars connected to your Soul and Fractal through the Golden Filaments. Able to play with other Free To Be Avatars. Free to create great wonders in the world of form. This is the realm of godlings.

This is the subject of our next chapter.

Contemplation and Journal section

What Teachings Resonated With Me in This Section?
Why?
How Does This Affect Me?

The Waves, You and Everything Else

This chapter at a glance:

- Negative Spaces.
- Why Closed Systems, Open Systems exist.
- You are One with All That Is.

ONE

Out of One.
Came All.
Therefore All are One.

The Waves, You and Everything Else

Creator permeates everything through the Golden Filaments. IT can behold suffering but IT cannot suffer. Suffering arises from an illusion of separation. God is Unity. The One is everywhere and all at once. There is nowhere where God isn't.

Can we find God in negative places?

Yes, the One is there too. Unholy darkness is simply a forgetting. A deep psychosis and a form of blindness. It is being in a room filled with shadows and not seeing the lamp. But the lamp exists nevertheless.

It is God.

In our multiverse there are entire Systems that are Open and entire Systems that are Closed. There are Systems on a vast spectrum in between. Every kind of System is in existence. One System is not better than another. They all serve a purpose.

When a Fractal wants to experience contraction it can dip into a more Closed System. When it wishes to expand it can dip into a more Open System. Fractals use three actions to experience themselves:

1. Expansion
2. Pause
3. Contraction

Fractals issue Avatars through a Soul in this sequence:

1. Thought (thought emerges).
2. Sound (issues a sound).
3. Light (a spark flares).
4. Compression (Soul).
5. Form (matter grows from the spark).

As Avatars we reflect this process in manifestation:

- We think (an idea emerges).
- We speak (talk about our idea).
- We imagine, create (a spark of energy arises around the idea).
- We compress our ideas (make a simplified plan).
- We execute (our idea takes form).

As we expand our consciousness we begin to understand that the Laws of Physics are elastic and can be manipulated. Linear Space Time operates like a railway track. It is fixed and offers three basic positions:

1. Back (past).
2. Pause (present).
3. Forward (future).

Gravity is what magnetizes human consciousness into Linear Space Time, pulling us down into a physical position. In order to resonate within the third-dimension a fragment of our Fractal's Frequencies are compressed and slowed down to give dimension to form. Our form is created before we are conceived within Earth's holographic simulation, and comes with a unique blueprint.

This experience is jarring and can give us a sensation of being stuck in a place where our options seem to be cast in iron. But this is an illusion. Our experiences are governed by the level of consciousness we can generate. We do that through raising our Frequencies.

Consciousness acts like an anti-gravitational device. We can levitate far beyond our perceived limitations and five sensory world like a bee. We can rise up above a flower's petaled head (our immediate reality) and see a vast field of blooms (the wider field of possibilities).

This is a Godly perspective.

Yet, God can also be found in the flower. IT embodies and inhabits every element and experiences the sensations of:

- Density
- Gravity
- Limitation
- Linear Time
- Space
- Taste
- Sound
- Sight
- Touch
- Smell

… through us and all creation.

When people say that *the devil is in the detail* they are in distortion, the Truth is, *God is in the detail*. There are countless dimensions for the God Consciousness to experience and inhabit. Each dimension folds into another like a Russian doll.

One dimension is not better than another. Just as one incarnation is not more valuable than another.

Whether it be an angel, an alien, a King, or an earthworm. They all carry value. All options are open to a Fractal because it embodies the Consciousness of the One. Therefore all experiences are equal.

Nature offers Open and Closed Systems. Instinct is a Closed System, because it is fixed and coded into the organism. But in every species are those that choose to awaken and rise out of instinctive behaviors.

You will see it in an animal's eyes. In fact, some species can be far more conscious than the average human. All creatures are capable of awakening. Everything pulses with potential. This is why every creature deserves to be treated with dignity.

Fractals can choose to be a star, a sun and any heavenly body. They can choose to become an element like the rain. Fractals can embody phenomena like a rainbow or lightning. They can become a Black Hole and devour entire solar systems.

All that needs to occur is an idea. And then the idea sprouts into a desire, a longing. The desire creates sound. The sound issues a command. The command casts the lightwaves. The lightwaves manifest form.

The form is blessed (approved of).
God saw that it was good.
And so it was.

Avatars do not possess the ability to instantly manifest reality. Gravity and density slow this process down, which is a safeguard. But Avatars do create their own realities, most often unconsciously. Our desires and thoughts set the process in motion. The outward effects take longer but the chain reaction is the same: the idea to desire to words to light to waves to reality.

Avatars can streamline this process through consciousness. Self-awareness unlocks enhanced skill sets, gifts and abilities. This comes as a natural consequence of Cleaning Up Our Space (Tenet 1) which in technical terms means to clear out our electromagnetic field. This allows our centrifugal/centripetal Sphere to spin faster within a stable structure. As velocity builds our electromagnetic field becomes more powerful.

This is the formula for Transfiguration.

Transfiguration transforms an Avatar into a godling*. Ascension is not an upward trajectory. It isn't an end destination. Otherwise where would it end?

A godling is a cocreator that is incubated until it reaches a required consciousness to instantaneously manifest matter.

Ascension is an expansion of consciousness that moves in any direction. It can involve descension or a "fall," which is Free Fall and complete surrender. What we are talking about here is movement. This is why illuminated masters choose to incarnate back on Earth. This reality is a fertile growth space.

Fractals can also hit pause and hibernate. They can be nothing and do nothing for eons at a time. They can choose to observe. When we remove the mechanism of Space Time the concept of getting somewhere vanishes. The idea of being someone disappears. This is because Time doesn't matter and being in a Space has no significance.

Space Time has no hold over a Fractal.

When Avatars enter the realms outside of Space Time and return to their Fractal, via their Soul, they experience a spherical existence. This is the full totality of existence like an ocean knowing itself, as opposed to through its parts as in a river or droplets.

In truth, we all dwell in the simultaneous ever-present Now. Where all Nows collapse into One Golden Now and we become one with all things.

This is Omniscience.
Everything in existence connected through the Golden Filaments to God.

All Fractals are connected to one another through God. Just as all Avatars are connected to their Fractal through their Soul. The Golden Filaments are a divine network. They map out everything in our cosmos. Resonating God consciousness in all things.

This is Omnipresence.

The Creator has no fixed location. Such as a throne in a palace in some lofty dimension. Creator is the consciousness that pulses through everything. Through our connection to God, to our Fractal, through our Soul, and to one another we too become omniscient, omnipresent.

How is this congruent with the darker realms and existences within our cosmos?

Hellish places are Closed Systems that continue to exist because they are activated by Avatar presence through Fractal curiosity. None of these places need to exist. They are places to go to experience low-resonating Frequencies. A Fractal's equivalent of "slumming it."

Another extreme sensation is bliss. Fractals have created great heavenly realms filled with every kind of delight and pleasure. There are many Avatars who choose to play, then slumber, then play again in these realms.

The desire to incarnate again and again into blissful renditions can be appealing. This appeal creates a strong electromagnetic field drawing aspects of the Fractal back. Epochs of bliss are as unfruitful as epochs of pain.

Maintaining a balance in our evolution path is the key.

The Soul is no minor player. A Fractal has many Souls. We can think of them as platforms of information, as sacred portals like the sun. Souls are intelligent and self-aware. A Soul has the capacity to host innumerable Avatars. There are no limitations to what a Fractal can process and access through its hub of Souls.

For an Avatar, a connection to its Soul is vital to consciousness. We can think of our Soul as a personal guide and our home town. It speaks to us through our hearts. It will feel like our intuition and is the source of our courage, and inspiration. It is a relationship we do well to cultivate. We can do this by trusting our intuition, our gut reactions and through spending regular time in stillness, solitude and in contemplation.

Remember, the Soul captures an emission of individuated Life Force released from a Fractal and compresses it. Incarnation into a third-dimensional reality as an Avatar requires this. Upon an Avatar's death the emission is expanded through an extraction technology and is resurrected back into the Soul. It is in this platform where Avatar's experiences are processed.

It is possible for a human Avatar who is clear enough, to be able to access many renditions of itself within its Soul while still alive in human form.

All of these other renditions are resonating in a Point of Now (P.O.N) but at different junctures of this third-dimensional reality. For example, we may have a rendition of ourselves that is 1) P.O.N 2024, and 2) P.O.N 1965 and 3) P.O.N 1876 and so forth.

Great masters can hold multiple P.O.N's simultaneously as a Golden Point of Now, which is a Godly perspective. To hold the experiences of such a number requires:

1. Discipline
2. Acceptance
3. High-Frequencies

4. A strong magnetic base
5. A clear centrifugal/centripetal Sphere
6. A stable velocity
7. Integrity
8. Unconditional Love
9. Unconditional Forgiveness

It is total awareness of everything one is everywhere and all at once. This ability comes with great responsibility. This type of Synthesis creates the equivalent of an Avatar SuperNova releasing an enormous amount of power and energy.

Such humans can expand and become powerful leaders. Unfortunately, many turn out to be despotic, parasitizing off the minions beneath them. Human history is littered with such people.

The Earth offers Avatars a choice between living in a Closed System and living in an Open System. Both can resonate simultaneously within the same planetary electromagnetic field. This is the reason why some humans dwell in bliss and others live in hell.

It could even be two people living in the same house. One resonates in Harmonic Resonance and the other resonates Incoherent Dissonance. Consequently, their experiences will be markedly different. Consciousness is the way out of a Closed System.

The Waves and the 8 Tenets offer us a trajectory for a stable, balanced expansion. It is designed to support Avatars leaving a Closed System for an Open System, but it is not the only way. The One is the Source of All. So, there are many ways out of a Closed System. You must follow your heart and find your path. No one is left behind.

Avatars were designed to evolve into godlings through *personal self-realization*. This is a State of Being that unites the human to its Soul, to its Fractal, and to God in the exact same epiphany moment of bliss.

This is Zero Point where Everything implodes into enlightenment through Oneness.

Evolution, revelation and transfiguration occurs in an infinite geometry of motion. Therefore, there is (potentially) as much enlightenment to be attained through descension into an Avatar or earthworm as there is in ascension back up into an Avatar to a Soul, to a Fractal to Creator.

All experiences are equal.
Experience creates reference points.
Reference points offer values.
Values confer meaning.
Meaning is subjective.

All creators in pursuit of experiences are ultimately questing for meaning. The greatest meaning we could ever find is derived through connection. This is a profound Truth.

Our lives have value and meaning fundamentally because of the people we love. Our Soul derives meaning and value due to a connection to its Avatars. Our Fractal discovers enormous meaning and value through its connection to Creator and to all of its Souls and Avatars.

Creator experiences bliss (meaning and value) through a connection to all creation.

Bliss (meaning and value) can only come through connection to God.

Contemplation and Journal section

What Teachings Resonated With Me in This Section?
Why?
How Does This Affect Me?

You and God

This chapter at a glance:

- How can we draw closer to God?
  - The effect of Gravity.
  - Gravity, Space and Time.
  - Free Fall.
- Embodiment, Surrender, Transfiguration.

You and God

In relation to the question, how can I draw closer to God? We need to first understand the role that gravity plays in consciousness. We know that gravity possesses a magnetic function that keeps all material objects in orbit with one another and in an orderly manner.

Gravity is also the force that slows Frequencies down. Human Avatars are located within a third-dimensional, holographic grid composed of Gravity, Space and Time. For this reason an Avatar's experiences are denser, last longer, and are more intense precisely because of gravity.

Gravity is what fixes you here and connects you to the Earth's core. We are held within her electromagnetic field. You possess gravity too as part of your electromagnetic field. The body's gravitational force bends Time in order to establish an Avatar's position in Space. To summarize, through Gravity, Space and Time you are held in place and can be located by all other beings.

You signal and receive Frequencies from this position within Space Time. So, you could move to the other side of the world but your actual Frequency position would remain the same. There is a natural consequence to this.

A third-dimensional rendition requires the compression of consciousness. Incarnation into matter concentrates the essence of a Fractal's consciousness into a human Avatar. Like a divine elixir, this essense holds all of the information of an Avatar's blueprint. Space Time and Gravity are compressant agents, but an expanded consciousness extracts the essence. This is the blossom of awakening.

Gravity provides a certain perspective, so that everything can be seen as having a beginning, a middle and an end; as having a start out and a destination point; as being a task or something to be mastered; as being studied and understood intellectually; as done, as being done or needing to be done. It is the perception of being separate from all other things.

That perspective is useful for everyday human activities like having relationships, raising children, and engaging in commerce but it cannot be applied to our spiritual existence. Our spiritual existence is beyond Space Time and Gravity.

It is not governed nor subject to the Laws of Physics and it cannot be processed from this perspective.

This is where we must abandon the intellect and surrender. We surrender to not-knowing and Free Fall into the divine mystery.

Free Fall opens up Tenet 5: Free To Be, to us

> "We do not operate from old paradigms. We are free of rituals, rites, orders and rank. We commune in equality. There is no hierarchy."

Surrender to the mystery of God liberates us from seeking and frees us from rituals. It relieves us of a mediator and delivers us from the burden of obedience and worship. Free

Fall opens us up to personal revelation and anoints us into the living words of God.

Free Fall opens us up to embodiment.

The great teachers understood this when they said that God dwells within you. We may ask, "Yes, but how can I feel closer to God? How do I connect?" In the asking of those questions did you notice how it opened up a space. A distance between you and God? That is an illusion.

The Truth is, you are already known fully to God. So, what we want to do here is pull out from within the evidence of a divine relationship. One that is already in existence. It is a relationship that you are hardwired and coded for.

A divine relationship collapses Space Time. It bends external Gravity to sync with our body's gravitational forces. This is why we say that consciousness is an anti-gravitational device. It pulls us out of the density of matter. It frees us from the perspective of separation to everything.

In this book we have learned that through our DNA we broadcast and we receive Frequencies. That our human bodies are an antenna. That we are all constantly communicating with one another. That our Golden Filaments connect to everything in creation. That we are an expression of our Fractal and that our Fractal is a reflection of God.

From a third-dimensional perspective it would be natural for us to see ourselves at the bottom of the ladder, as a pawn on the chessboard and as a small puppet Avatar on the end of a golden string. One amongst countless other puppet Avatars that are all tethered to a giant luminous mothership Fractal.

That in turn is connected to innumerable other mothership Fractals that are connected through a vast network of Golden Filaments to a gigantic ball of brilliant light - that is God.

Can you feel the distance between everything that that implies?

What if I told you that everything folds into you? That you contain the entire multiverse? How would that shift things for you? This can feel like the rug being pulled from under you. It can feel like free-falling through a massive chasm not being able to hold onto anything.

How could we be everything?

What if every idea humans have had about the Creator is a distortion? This may not feel comfortable.

The Truth isn't comfortable. Transfiguration is about letting go of everything we thought was true. A godling represents the embodiment of God made flesh. This is not blasphemous. It is a Truth that has been concealed from us by those who want to control the human race.

The Truth is less that we need to seek God and more that we need to embody God.

- The Prime Cause.
- The One.

Embodiment is Surrender.
Surrender is Transfiguration.
Transfiguration is Connection.
Connection is Bliss (meaning + value).

How can we support Transfiguration? There are many ways. Nature will bring you into alignment every single time. Living as closely to natural rhythms will reinforce your Godliness. Meditating upon and practicing unconditional love will bring you into a Godly resonance.

There are other absolutes that hold no opposites and exemplify God:

- Truth
- Purity

The latter being a state of clarity like a perfectly cut diamond. The search for God therefore is the search for ourselves. To find God is to find ourselves. Instead of asking where God is, we can ask where am I right now, in this moment? Where am I in every moment? For where you truly are, God is.

So, can we experience God directly and individually? Yes. Kaya Usher is the Teacher's Teacher and in 2019, she was shown a body of teachings that facilitate a return Home (within) to God. The message she received was simple: God never left us.

God has always been here, waiting patiently for us to remember that separation from the One is an illusion. And that this illusion came about because first we were separated from ourselves. When you separate from yourself, you pull away from God who dwells within.

If you come back fully into your body and Clean Up that Space you will experience God more fully.

If you go into stillness, you will hear God. If you let go of control and Free Fall, God will appear to you in innumerable manifestations.

> *"The Simplicity Platform - 8 Tenets* is a technology of letting go. For us godlings it's about trust and then letting go. For Creator there is no need of trust. Creator lets go perpetually." Kaya Usher Free To Be 365

If we want to experience God more deeply we must become what we seek. It is never outside of ourselves. To find God we must become Godly. Direct communion with God is there for you. You are hard-wired for personal revelation and miracles.

When we seek God within we must let go of all attachments to outcome. That which we seek with a need attached to it, is pushed away from us like the chasing of a butterfly or a leaf blown about by the wind.

Seek not therefore for an experience outside of yourself. Surrender, detach and stay in the ever-present Now, which is full embodiment with the flesh. That's where God dwells.

Creator holds the space for communion in the flesh and is playful. Daily, we can say aloud, "I wonder how God will surprise me today?" and then we let go and get on with our day.

When an animal gazes sweetly into your eyes behold the presence of God. When you feel the rain upon your skin behold the presence of God. When you have prevailed through a challenging time behold the presence of God. With every breath that you take behold the presence of God.

When a kind word is needed, become the presence of God. When help is sought by a stranger, become the presence of God. When the weak are oppressed, become the presence of God. When it seems to many that all hope is lost, become the presence of God.

This is a dynamic space. You are a divine partner. The Creator delights in ITS creation. You are the literal meaning of the term

I AM

You are the presence of the Living God. What then, is the difference between an Avatar and a godling?

You are.

It has always been You.
That is Transfiguration.

Thank you for joining us on this pathway.

Ours is a sacred relationship and we would like to close with a prayer. It has been adapted from a prayer in Kaya Usher's book *Free To Be 365*.

A prayer is a conversation with God. It wasn't intended to be a vibration of want, or a petition, or an out-pouring of guilt and self-remorse. It is an offering of Frequencies. The invitation to entangle and co-create. So we can treat our prayers as an opportunity to connect with our Creator more deeply.

We offer this prayer not as a model, or as a how-to, but as a gift of expression. We invite you to join with your Creator in a manner that feels good to you.

GOD,

I AM here for you, with you, made from you.
I AM here to flow with you in the highest order.
I ask that the purest most holy space
opens for us to receive any knowledge
that will aid your godling.

I AM your signal.
I AM your messenger.
I AM your Lightning Rod.
I AM opened up now, with you, of you.
In your Holy name bring in the highest order.
Keep me grounded.
I stand before you unwavering in my devotion.
I thank you.

And so it is.

Contemplation and Journal section

What Teachings Resonated With Me in This Section?
Why?
How Does This Affect Me?

Activation: Grounding Golden Sovereign Technique

We close The Waves but the work continues.
We use everything as a tool, a technique to know ourselves even more deeply.

The Grounding Golden Sovereign Technique is an excellent practice for clearing ourselves after we have spent a lot of time with others. Perhaps, through work-related events or family get-togethers over the holiday when it's easy to get entangled. This technique is also useful for when we feel triggered or overwhelmed. It will gently guide us back more fully into ourselves.

Our mother, the Earth, is always there for us.

Get comfortable.
Please close your eyes and see your natural inanimate objects in your mind's eye.
You now embody the gifts of those teachers.
They are entraining you through stillness.
They are guiding you through humility.
They are showing you through service.
(Pause)

We hold the Light of God.
We are as solid as a Rock.
We are as light as a feather.
(Pause)

Grounding ...
Grounded to the Earth.

Golden ...
Filled with the Golden Filaments.

Sovereign ...
Our system belongs to us and us alone.

Technique ...
Our technique to use always.

Count down from 33 to zero,
gently disconnect from the Group field,
and drop more deeply into your Avatar.
Feel that.

(Count down softly)
33 32 31 30 29 28 27 26 25 24 23 22 21
20 19 18 17 16 15 14 13 12 11
10 9 8 7 6 5 4 3 2 1 - Zero

See yourself as a Frequency light being,
generating a brilliant dazzling light that beams out to form
a golden electromagnetic field.
You see a giant, glowing ball in the distance.
Is it the sun?
No, it is our Earth.
you are seeing her as a Frequency being.

She is radiant, luminous.
Her Sphere glows within a brilliant gridwork of light.
The Frequency field she projects is enormous.
It feels warm.
It feels inviting.
You can hear a faint pulse like a heartbeat.
With each pulse the grid is lit up.
In between the pulse it glows a little softer.

There's a magnetic pull.
It feels like love.
Now, walk towards her.
Feel her warmth.
Feel her light.
You enter her electromagnetic field.
You stop at her center.
It feels like a warm blanket, a burrow to curl up in.
Even though her electromagnetic field is bright, here - here, it is dark and soothing.
It smells like the hearth, of soft soil, of wood, of rain.

Stretch out your arms and legs and touch the luminous lines you feel all about you.
Feel our Earth connect to your Golden Filaments.
Feel that surge of Frequencies.
It lights you up.
It fills your body.
And yet, you are held in the comforting darkness of her core.
The gentle beat of her heart.

Boom Boom Boom Boom
Safe - connected - activated - grounded.
Be here always.

Reflections on Transfiguration

Ponder on the following or create some concepts from Section 3 in the following notes section.

"Unconditional forgiveness releases everyone involved from a Closed Circuit. So, if one player wakes up, the unconscious game is over."
Do you feel the ripple effect of how we are all connected?

"Our experiences are governed by the level of consciousness we can generate."
What does this mean to you?

"The Truth is, you are already known fully to God."
Sit with this truth. Feel what comes up for you.

Practice Ideas:

- Spend as much time in nature as possible, no matter the weather. Feel the natural clearing that occurs when you are submersed in nature.
- Practice the game of saying "I wonder how God will surprise me today?" and then let go. Take note throughout the day of all the blessings, be they big or small, that were gifted to you.
- If it feels true for you, practice the Grounding Golden Sovereign Technique at the end of the day before you fall asleep. This will untangle your energy from people, places, and things you encountered throughout your day and will fold your energy back into just you.

Separation is an illusion. Your connection to God is already there, patiently waiting for you. This divine relationship is your birthright.

Contemplation and Journal section

The Waves Endnotes:

Book Assets

Closing Thoughts 181
What Others are Experiencing 189
About Kaya Usher 191
Guide to Using this Book 193
Glossary of Terms 201
Diagram List 209
Useful Links 211

CLOSING THOUGHTS

Your life is the consequence of your Frequencies expressed in waves. Take time to regularly check in. How do you feel about your present environment? What does your life (experience) feel like, day in and day out? Would you change anything about your life NOW? Ponder as much on your feelings as on your thoughts. Take notes and time out from your life schedule for reflection.

If there's a gap between your current life experience and what you wish for, know that that gap is the consequence of incoherence in your electromagnetic field. Your electromagnetic field is where you signal (Push) and draw (Pull) from.

An incoherent electromagnetic field manifests as mental and emotional instability. It can produce a life that feels chaotic. With good things happening randomly, and not-so-good things happening randomly too.

A person with incoherence often blames life, the elements outside of themselves and beyond their control. Ultimately, the turmoil is manufactured within them and then resonated out in waves. The individual is literally projecting their chaos out in waves which creates more disorder.

Do you feel that life is something that happens to you? Do you believe that you have no control over it? Learn to turn that around. Own everything that comes your way because you are co-creating those experiences. You are *that* powerful.

On first appearance, it does appear that life is an outside-in experience. That humans are impacted by their world, more than they impact it. This is because life on Earth is dynamic. It isn't a holiday destination.

Everything in creation is in motion, in vibration. Every cell in your body is resonating. Every system, every organ is experiencing movement. Turbulence, flux and flow are natural. This doesn't magically change when we come into coherence.

What changes is our interaction with the dynamic forces of creation.

So, The Waves won't flatten the ups and downs of your life out and usher in a personal Utopia. What it will do is to help you stop fighting life, to stop reacting to it, to drop all resistance to it. It will teach you how to surf the dynamic waves of life. The key is to have a stable, internal velocity while experiencing the energetic pace of existence.

The Waves will bring you into a deeper state of consciousness, of awareness. This is particularly important because according to cognitive neuroscientists, the average human is conscious around five percent of their cognitive activity. That means most decisions, actions, emotions, and behavior, depend upon the ninety-five percent of brain activity that is unconscious.

Currently, the majority of humans live unconsciously. This collective, unconscious mode of living is reflected out into our world, which in turn feels unconscious, erratic, impulsive. In its darkest forms, collective unconsciousness generates war, greed, violence, pollution, disease and famine.

Due to the high volume of humans alive today (more than at any other time) the collective unconscious is burdening our Earth. Collective unconsciousness also presents a challenge for conscious humans. It infringes upon their ability to thrive. We must return back to a place of balance.

The good news is that the higher Frequencies always override the lower Frequencies. This means that it takes less conscious people to balance out the more unconscious people. Coherence is more impactful than incoherence.

Make this a daily Practice
Observe what is being generated by your electromagnetic field, right now. Note any shifts in moods and feelings.

- Pause.
- Observe (Without judgment).
- Note.

Are there areas that feel unbalanced, turbulent, impulsive, random or repetitive? Are you looping the same experiences over and over again?

Ask: Where is the incoherence in my electromagnetic field? Show me.

The Waves will reveal things to you in numerous ways. Each set of revelations are particular to the student. For some, feelings in the body can signal feedback. For others, it may come in the form of dreams. There may be coincidences, lightbulb moments, or observations made from others. A book or movie may come a student's way. An animal may embody a message from our Fractal.

The key is to remain open to all possibilities.

Learn to *regularly* check in with yourself. Interrupt unconsciousness (habits, distractions, behaviors, traits) through present-moment awareness. Stay in your body. Use breathwork. Use nature. Go barefoot. Stay aware of every trigger. For in truth, they are gifts.

Observe how unconsciousness pulls you in. Watch how daydreams suck you back into sleepwalking. Irritability can be a distraction technique too, as can the sudden on-set of boredom. Watch your fantasies and points of interest. Follow your thoughts with the determined focus of a detective. Feel when your awareness is being pulled out of the present-moment.

Ask: What pulled me?

Ask: Where did I just go?

Only the present-moment is conscious. Everything else (the past, the future) is unconscious. All programs (habits, beliefs, traits, biases, behaviors) are unconscious. All addictions are unconscious.

Observe your dreams, journal, doodle them out. You can use the My Notes pages in this book to document your observations. Pay close attention to how you feel upon waking. All random thoughts and feelings expressed in dreams are a window into your unconscious. Dreams can reveal much about our family programs, our lineage.

Ask before you go to sleep: show me where I can expand even further.
Ask when you wake: What do my dreams reveal?
The Waves will show you.

Caveat: As with all observations (daytime, sleeptime) never judge yourself.

Embodiment = present-moment.
Present-moment = embodiment.

There are other techniques, substances, gurus and sacred places on Earth that people use to hack their consciousness. But those pathways are often short lived, because they are third-party. This is your work to do and cannot be outsourced without a penalty of sovereignty being paid.

Hear Truth.

The Frequency of need and of fear disrupts. It creates a disturbance in our electromagnetic field. This magnetizes more experiences of lack, of need, of wanting more. But if we let go, and accept our experience, as it resonates now. If we stop signaling waves of need or want, our electromagnetic field will begin to clear. It will come back into balance, and into neutrality which is the realm of all possibilities.

Then, the "I AM" space of all possibilities will emerge.

Spend time feeling the Earth's Frequency system. Our planet resonates in pulses like a human heart and staying connected to her will keep you grounded throughout the course of reading this book.

Now hold or look at your partners in creation, that is, natural inanimate objects.

Look at them.
Hold them.
Feel them.

They are your guides as you navigate The Waves. They are present to remind you of your own deep resonance: solid, perfect and pure. Feel the Frequencies they run. They are tethered to our Earth.

Ask these partners in creation to show you how to be: *As solid as a rock and as light as a feather.* If we were to observe our waves in Harmonic Resonance that would be the formula. For Lightness of Being = a clear electromagnetic field, and as Solid as a Rock = grounded, tethered to our Earth.

Remember ….
You came to resonate waves and shift your reality.
It isn't the other way around.

How to use the five Waves

1. Harmonic Resonance (bring yourself into a state of coherence)
2. Emergence (observe everything that comes up)
3. Osmosis (embody "feel" all components)
4. Transfiguration (bring all parts into Synthesis)
5. Grounding Golden Sovereign Technique (bring everything back to mother Earth)

WHAT OTHERS ARE EXPERIENCING

"I was first introduced to Kaya via a tap-in session, which was profound in terms of tuning in to my body. This led me directly to reading the book The Simplicity Platform. I devoured it and was really hungry for more frequency work and to connect to others interested in this work. Not too long after that the course The Waves was offered I really felt called to sign up for it.

I was uncertain of where it would lead me but what I found was that each and every class resonated really deeply within me. Some of what was covered in the courses I had experienced before. In meditation or through other practices or study, I just didn't have language for it or understand how it all connected. Now I do! … The connection and understanding that was happening in my body was quite profound and changed me." A.G

"Letting what doesn't make cognitive sense just be, and bringing a patience to myself, are ways I've opened to The Waves, and stewarded my own receptivity to their impact.

My experience reflects that the process unfolds regardless, and there is an inevitability to shifting, but I would call Trust highly catalyzing — however one can embody or practice it. Felt gains in stability, momentum and power come in more tightly with Trust, but the dissolution of inner resistance quickens too. There's tangibly new terrain available, inside a surrender of this sort." L.M

"The Waves have brought awareness to parts of my life where I am unconscious. It is guiding me to consciousness in my daily life and in my dreams. The most profound shift that the waves have caused in my human and spirit form is forgiving all the splintered parts of myself and bringing them back into One as I expand." A.C

"The Waves teaching has opened me up into a deeper dive of who I am and why I am here. The information given so beautifully by Kaya felt like a deep remembering of knowledge I had once known but somehow forgot. Most importantly, it helped me unlock within myself a stable velocity, a steady momentum. Which is something I had been working on continuously with the 8 Tenets. The Waves teachings felt like the missing key to my acceleration and embodiment." E.S

ABOUT KAYA USHER

Kaya Usher was born in Toronto, Canada. In her twenties she went to University, met and fell in love with Gord Downie. They married and went on to have four children. As Downie's career took off, Usher stayed home and raised their family.

Later, in her mid-forties through a series of devastating personal challenges Kaya Usher awakened. She received a body of knowledge called The Simplicity Platform 8 Tenets, a Frequency Technology that when practiced activates a profound embodied enlightenment and physical coherence.

As the Teacher's Teacher, Kaya Usher shares this Frequency Technology to students from all over the world through a collection of books, courses and music.

A GUIDE TO USING THIS BOOK

The Waves technology is embodiment. We ask that you allow your body to have feelings, and sensations around this material. We ask that you observe your thoughts, as well as your doubts - let them roll in and roll out, like ocean waves. Our focus will be inside of our body. We will Free Fall into stillness and let silence be our guide.

The Waves is a central component of The Simplicity Platform - 8 Tenets technology. It is an enhanced velocity system that operates through, within and around the 8 Tenets. It was first revealed in Kaya Usher's Daily Word book Free To Be 365 which is frequently quoted throughout this book. Any or all of the below will orient students:

Immersion (pre-recorded course)
The Simplicity Platform 8 Tenets (book)
The Practice Student Workbook (book)
Free To Be 365 (book)
The Waves (pre-recorded course)
(Go to thesimplicityplatform.com/store for purchasing details)

For convenience we have included a Glossary of Terms following this section.

The Simplicity Platform 8 Tenets represent Kaya Usher's foundational teachings and were revealed to her in 2019. She is the Teacher's Teacher. The Waves build upon these teachings. One does not replace the other. The 8 Tenets remain the guiding principles, and we recommend that you continue with your own practice of them.

Understanding the role of The Simplicity Platform 8 Tenets in your life will enhance it. That is beyond question. The Tenets teach us how Frequencies work and The Waves represent the next step in mastering your life experience.

This body of knowledge rolls out in eight protocols:

Tenet 1 : Clean Up Your Space (pull up any distortions that are hampering your life)

> "Our space is a sovereign state. When we incarnate into a physical body, we pick up junk: inherited programs, familial and ethnic customs, societal and cultural habits. None of which is us. Our first act of freedom is, therefore, to "unlearn" everything that isn't us and jettison it from our space."

Tenet 2 : Ride The Truth Wave (understand how distortions came to exist and your role in them)

> "With truth comes freedom. We are free to be ourselves – not different versions dependent on who we are with. Our truth is unique to us and its hallmark is integrity."

Tenet 3 : Come Home To Your Most Brilliant Self (actively let go of what is not you)

> "The greatest love of all – is our love for self. Without it we cannot love another. Once we are free to love ourselves unconditionally, we are able to love all things."

Tenet 4 : Usher In An Unimaginable Peace (an inner condition that comes with release work)

> "There is only one peace and that is within. Once we enter into our sovereignty, in peace, we can externalize it into the world."

Tenet 5 : Live Free To Be (you experience more freedom, worry less)

> "We do not operate from old paradigms. We are free of rituals, rites, orders and rank. We commune in equality. There is no hierarchy."

Tenet 6 : Sustain Your Frequency (you discern the need for a daily routine and develop one)

> "We dwell in a neutral space, neither swayed this way or that. In staying centered, grounded, we maintain our frequency equilibrium."

Tenet 7 : Live Inside The Simplicity Platform (you open up more possibilities, you stay in the Now)

"There are no more stories, complexities, doubts, debates or emergencies. Our lives become simpler. We stay in the present moment. Always connected."

Tenet 8 : Embody The Lightness of Being (you are fully in your body, stay present, resonate light)

"We enter into the realm of spontaneous gifts. Miraculous events, inconceivable adventures and exchanges of gifts replace the old world of money, work and contracts."

When you complete one cycle of the 8 Tenets, it's recommended that you take three weeks off for integration, essentially this means that you take a break from the practice. Then, you repeat the cycle again for another eight weeks, and so on.

The point of this is two-fold. First to build up momentum. Second, repetition induces depth. Momentum and depth produces present-moment embodiment. It took us time to realize this.

After working a few cycles of the 8 Tenets our students began to notice that an internal coherence came about. This was accompanied by a deep calm or peace and a more P.O.N (Point of Now) present-moment awareness.

Meaning that students had already Cleaned Up Their Space (1), were already resonating Truth (2), had known Brilliance and had Come Home to Themselves (3), had experienced Peace (4), knew how to live Freely (5), were Sustaining Themselves (6) and understood The Simplicity Platform

(7). This culminated in a state of perpetual Embodiment and Lightness (8).

Once a student understood how to run the 8 Tenets as one unified system, their electromagnetic field became more primed to run The Waves technology. And so, the difference between The Waves and the 8 Tenets is system bandwidth.

We use the 8 Tenets to open up a grounded space, and then we apply The Waves.

Structure

This book operates in three Sections with pauses in between for integration.

1. Section 1: Emergence = three chapters + spaces for integration, reflection and note-taking.
2. Section 2: Osmosis = six chapters + spaces for integration, reflection and note-taking.
3. Section 3: Transfiguration = three chapters + spaces for integration, reflection and note-taking.

Through the course of this book you will learn the connection between your Frequencies as expressed in waves and the wider community of other beings and their waves.

- The nourishing Void.
- Creator.
- Cosmos Frequency Field.
- Electromagnetic fields.
- Gravity.
- Velocity.

- Space Time.
- Others.

The Waves is written in the style that it was received. The information came in a poetic form and aside from some organization for clarity, we have not interfered with that pattern.

Suggested actions

We offer suggestions throughout this book that we believe will enhance your experience.

Pause

In the first Section you will see the word pause in parenthesis following each paragraph. This is a suggestion to stop and take in what you have just read, to ponder, and to observe mental or bodily reactions to a concept offered. In the second Section onward there will simply be a gap between paragraphs which offers you the opportunity to pause and reflect.

Blank spaces

There are spaces left blank in this book that we recommend you use for reflection and integration. You will learn to appreciate silence, and stillness through blankness. This allows you to drop out of your head space. Words often keep us outside of our bodies. We also suggest you take your time reading. Stop if need be and ponder. Take a break if you need to. Go at your own pace.

Inventory

There are areas of the book where statements, questions and concepts are offered for contemplation.

My Notes

These are spaces where you can organize your thoughts, experiences or epiphanies with The Waves.

Reflection

These are junctures dedicated to personal reflection of specific areas of The Waves teachings.

Frequency Partners

Before reading this book we recommend finding some things to partner with from the natural world. It could be a stone, a feather, a rock, an acorn or pine cone, a beeswax candle, a plant or even a glass of water. It could be one or a collection of things.

Do pets count? No, our animal companions are not inanimate; if anything, they are highly animated and are affected by our Frequencies. So what we are looking for here are inanimate natural objects.

The principles we will study are already embodied perfectly by these natural objects. Simply being in the presence of them will entrain us. We will be learning to feel the Frequencies of so-called inanimate objects. I invite you to keep those objects close to you as you read this book.

We do not recommend the use of crystals for this book and course. Crystals hold a tremendous amount of energy and can affect our Frequency field positively and negatively. The Waves is all about self-mastery. We do not seek magnification from a third party. Magnification always comes from within.

Take Your Time

The Waves is an exacting Frequency Technology and it will trigger changes in your life, which can create discomfort at times. It is designed to flag up your weak spots and the areas you need to let go of. If the work becomes too intense we recommend you put the book down until you feel ready to continue.

Join Our Community

You are not alone on this journey. Join other students of Kaya Usher's Frequency Technology here: thesimplicityplatform.com/the-simplicity-platform-community.

GLOSSARY OF TERMS

The nourishing Void
The Great and Holy Mystery beyond comprehension and yet everything that will ever be, has ever been and is in existence comes from the nourishing Void. Everything comes from the nourishing Void and returns to it.

God / Creator / Source / the Something / Prime Cause
The Origin of all things in our cosmos.

Eternal Flame
The essence of God, which is holy, luminescent and eternal and fuels Life Force.

The Golden Filaments
A sentient network that connects all living things to one another, forming a lattice of One. Snowflakes, silk threads and spider's webs offer the closest visuals for this phenomenon. They glow effervescent and are luminous, lit from within by God's Eternal Light.

An Avatar contains a network of Golden Filaments that are local to the human body.

Holy Waters
A substance that permeates the entire Cosmos that has yet to be understood. It is a Frequency rich plasma that acts like the waters in a uterus that support a growing fetus. Everything is held within these Holy Waters of God. The Golden Filaments are woven throughout these Holy waters.

Fractal / Spirit
This book uses the word Fractal in place of Spirit. A Fractal is a reflection of God and contains the same essense and abilities as its Creator. This is the infinite, non-local You as opposed to the third-dimensional localized Avatar you. Fractal / Spirit exists outside of Space Time and uses anti-gravity and leverages Zero Point, and is assessed in the present moment.

Soul
A sentient multidimensional platform that connects our Fractal / Spirit to its many Avatars. It is the mediator between non-physical and physical. Your soul holds more than one human Avatar at a time and more than one lifetime at a time. Your soul is not the same as your Fractal / Spirit.

Avatar
Your local self here on Earth. Your human Avatar is a questing agent for its Fractal. It exists within Space Time, and journeys towards self-realization through experiences.

Godling
A co-creator in training; a human Avatar that is awakened.

Blueprint / blueprint
Your Fractal's divine seal granted from inception by God. An inner plan within a human bestowed by its Fractal.

Imprint

Fractals gather Imprints through their Avatars. Imprints hold experiences and patterns of belief and behaviors that are passed down generation to generation, through a lineage and other lives (past, future). Avatars are also Imprinted in the course of life through people, places, things.

Splinter / Fragmentation

If a Fractal or Avatar experiences an extreme trauma in one or more lifetimes it can split and lose a part of itself. That part does not return through the Soul after death and can become trapped just outside of the Earth plane.

Most of us have had lives where we have experienced negative extremes and have therefore lost parts of ourselves. The Waves help to pull those fragmented splinters back in for Osmosis and Synthesis.

The Simplicity Platform 8 Tenets

Kaya Usher's foundational Frequency Technology that supports a stable internal velocity. We study this knowledge in cycles.

The Waves

The Waves demystifies the human experience and works as a powerful cleansing agency. It pulls from our unconscious / subconscious anything that has been hidden to us. This particular Technology flows continuously in five Frequency waves:

1. Harmonic Resonance.
2. Emergence.
3. Osmosis.

4. Transfiguration.
5. Grounding Golden Sovereign Technique.

Harmonic Resonance

A technique to bring yourself into attunement that produces a balanced, stable velocity orbit within as you open up to cleansing. Consequences are a profound state of peace and coherence in the electromagnetic field. The latter of which allows for a clear singular signal (push) and a clear magnetic draw (pull).

Emergence

A state of profound self-awareness and observation of previously obscured or hidden elements that require release or integration. These elements arise from our subconscious and the Spheres of our existence where humans normally have limited access.

Osmosis

A state of reconnection to previously hidden or blocked elements. This is a feeling space. We feel first through our heart and our bodies and then we process through our headspace. This can sometimes be challenging and uncomfortable. We absorb what is useful and we release what is not. This is a holistic process.

Transfiguration

A state of embodiment where we bring in all of the elements of Imprints into our blueprint through Synthesis. (embodiment + synthesis = transfiguration)

Grounding Golden Sovereign Technique
A technique where we release everything to mother Earth and her Golden Filaments. This helps to ground us and keeps us stable and feeling light.

Embodiment
The process whereby an Avatar's Fractal fully or more fully inhabits that individual's human body. It also denotes the state whereby an individual *becomes* something of high-Frequency, ie: Truth, Love, Integrity, Peace.

Free Fall
An act of personal surrender; a letting go of all attachment, wants and expectations.

The Physics of Creation
An entire universe comes into existence through these principles:

1. Out of nothing comes something.
2. Separation is loss, risk and Free Fall into Fractals that push individuation.
3. Everything returns to nothing.

These are the fundamentals.

The Three Spheres
Humans experience three realms simultaneously: awake time, sleeping time referred to in this book as the "Dreamscape" and the places before birth and after death via their connection to their Fractal. Our P.O.N (Point of Now) consciousness resides in the intersected center of these three Spheres.

The Principles: Avatar mechanics
These principles govern five areas of the human body:

1. Spiritual
2. Physical
3. Emotional
4. Sexual
5. Mental

Sphere (spinning)
A structure within each living being that resembles a golden, luminous Sphere. This Sphere spins (like a spinning top, with rotating wheels within wheels) generating a Frequency field and waves through velocity.

Centrifugal / Centripetal
Two components with our Sphere that generate velocity and momentum from within our electromagnetic field. Our centrifugal / centripetal Sphere sustains our Life Force, our Soul, our Fractal and our human body. Combined the centrifugal and centripetal motions create velocity. This structure is powered by our Life Force, which is the essence of God.

Waves
Frequencies move in waves. We are composed of waves. Like actual ocean waves, waves flow either coherently or incoherently. Waves carry information.

Velocity
The rate at which our Frequencies resonate waves determines how far we can expand, think: consciousness bandwidth.

Momentum
How stable our velocity generates waves determines our Harmonic Coherence, think: coherence.

Electromagnetic Field
This is a magnetized electric field that is generated by a human body through a totality of systems: brain, heart, digestive, etc. This field affects, and is affected by gravity. Frequencies resonate waves to and from this field.

Frequency Partners
Things to partner with that can teach us how to resonate waves in alignment with nature. It could be a stone, a feather, a rock, an acorn or pine cone, a beeswax candle, a plant or even a glass of water. It could be one or a collection of things.

Pulse
Electromagnetic fields generate and receive pulses. It is the compression then release of energy through Zero Point. Everything pulses.

26,000 Year Pulse
Every twenty-six thousand years a powerful pulse resonates from Zero Point (the Frequency center of the universe), like a tsunami, and it activates great resets and quantum leaps in evolution. We can think of it as the Creator's heartbeat.

Zero Point (the Frequency center of the universe)
The event horizon where all matter, energy and light collapses into and explodes from. It is an entry point to, and exit portal from the nourishing Void.

Point of Now (P.O.N)
This is when we bring our full attention into the present moment and are not distracted by the past or the future. It is being in sync with Space Time, much as animals and small children are.

Space Time
The location of an individual within a third-dimensional reality. It is where they resonate and signal from within the local and nonlocal Frequency Field. Space Time can be impacted (curved, compacted, etc) through consciousness.

Timeline
The product of an individual's choices, beliefs and actions. A timeline moves through an individual. An individual does not move along a timeline.

Gravity
A magnetic force that holds things (people, animals, planets, etc) in secure orbits, however, it can be impacted (curved, compacted) through consciousness. Gravity slows Frequencies down which enables a Fractal's Avatar to compress into physical matter. Gravity also holds us within Space and within Time.

Personal Immersion
A routine that supports and sustains an individual's Frequency health and equilibrium.

DIAGRAM LIST

Diagram 1: "Frequencies," copyright Kaya Usher Unlimited 2022.

Diagram 2: "Energy centers," copyright Kaya Usher Unlimited 2022.

Diagram 3: "DNA" copyright i-stock 2023.

Diagram 4: "Fractal" copyright i-stock 2023.

Diagram 5: "Soul" copyright i-stock 2023.

Diagram 6: "Human Node Network" copyright i-stock 2023.

USEFUL LINKS

Kaya Usher's websites
thesimplicityplatform.com
kayausher.com

The Simplicity Platform Community
thesimplicityplatform.com
the-simplicity-platform-community

Kaya Usher's platforms
facebook.com/thekayausher
instagram.com/thesimplicityplatform
twitter.com/thekayausher
youtube.com/@kayausherunlimited

Kaya Usher's books
amazon.com/Simplicity-Platform-Harness-Power-Frequencies (foundational work)
amazon.com/Free-Be-365-Frequency-Technology (daily word)
amazon.com/Practice-Journal-Kaya-Usher (workbook)

Contact Kaya Usher
contact@kayausher.com

Media queries
media@kayausher.com

Milton Keynes UK
Ingram Content Group UK Ltd.
UKHW020816090124
435677UK00001B/12